expect the
EXTRAORDINARY

expect the
EXTRAORDINARY

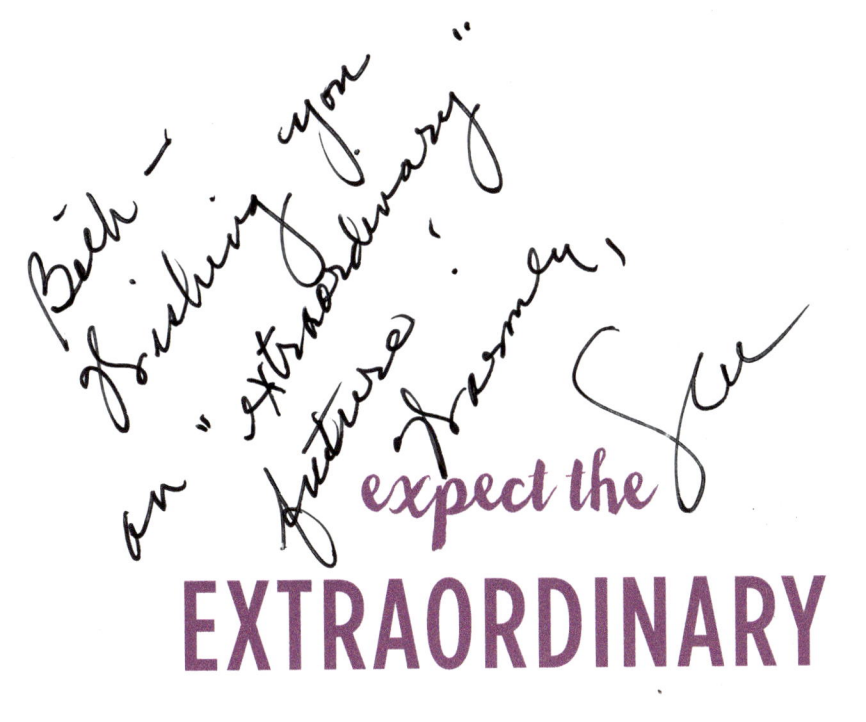

*Angelic Messages,
Spiritual Encounters,
and the Soul of Skye*

SUE PIGHINI

Livin' the Dream Media
Fredericksburg, Virginia

Copyright © 2016 by Sue Kipperman Pighini
All rights reserved under the International and Pan-American Copyright Conventions. Unless otherwise noted, no part of this book may be reproduced, stored in a retrieval system, or transmitted in any form or by any means, electronic, mechanical, photocopying, or otherwise, without the express written permission of the publisher, except for brief quotations or critical reviews. For more information, contact the author/publisher at www.livinthedreamranch.com.

Livin' the Dream Media, Fredericksburg, VA.

At the time of this book's publication, all facts and figures cited within are the most current available. All telephone numbers, addresses, and website URLs are accurate and active; all publications, organizations, websites, and other resources exist as described in this book. If you find an error or believe that a resource listed here is not as described, please contact the author/publisher.

Photo credits:
Back cover: www.picsofyou.com.
Interior credits on corresponding pages.

Editors: Diane Chesson and John Kober
Project management: Hobie Hobart, dunn-design.com
Cover design: Kathi Dunn, dunn-design.com
Interior design: Dorie McClelland, springbookdesign.com

ISBN: 978-0-9971638-1-0 (softcover)

Publisher's Cataloging-in-Publication
(Provided by Quality Books, Inc.)

    Pighini, Sue, author.
        Expect the extraordinary : angelic messages,
    spiritual encounters and the soul of Skye / Sue Pighini.
        pages cm
        ISBN 978-0-9971638-1-0

        1. Spiritual life--New Age movement.
        2. Self-actualization (Psychology)--Religious aspects.
        3. Angels. 4. Horses--Religious aspects. I. Title.

    BP605.N48P545 2016   299'.93
                    QBI16-600031

Printed in the United States of America

This book and its message of loving angelic connection is dedicated to those who are striving to live the life they dreamed of, and deeply desire to know that they are not alone. There is always hope for each of us—never, ever give up.

To those who are facing life's challenges including my 94-year-old mother, Candy, and my brother, Mike, I dedicate this book with the deepest admiration for your courage. You are all so loved and admired.

Contents

Preface *ix*
Introduction *xi*

Part I
My Angelic Encounters

Chapter 1   Whisper 1: Near death on an Arizona mountainside   *3*

Chapter 2   Whisper 2: Divine intervention in New York City   *9*

Chapter 3   Whisper 3: Cancer in Connecticut   *13*

Part II
Others' Life Saving Stories

Chapter 4   Scott's Near Death Experience   *21*

Chapter 5   Donnie's conversation with God   *27*

Part III
Finally Found It . . . A Formula for Greater Fearless Living

Chapter 6   Journey from corporate America to spiritual seeker   *37*

Chapter 7   How my life changed and how yours can too   *39*

Chapter 8   Tool 1: Positivity—How healthy are your cells?   *43*

Chapter 9   Tool 2: Ten Sacred Insights   *49*

Chapter 10 Tool 3: The Law of Attraction   *55*

Chapter 11 Get out of your comfort zone   *59*

Part IV
Where Am I Today?

Chapter 12 From heartbeats to hoofbeats: discovering my age of authenticity   *67*

Chapter 13 The experts speak   *77*

Chapter 14 The angels continue to amaze   *95*

Epilogue   *103*
Acknowledgements   *109*
Resources   *111*
About the author   *113*

Preface

As I finish writing this book, I ask myself why I felt so compelled to write about angelic conversations and the soul of a horse. I have had heart-to-heart chats with these divine messengers buried in my psyche for forty years. Why come out now with these revelations?

After working with hundreds of clients over the last twenty years as a Life Transition Coach, I came to realize that most of us live with some type of fear on a daily basis. I know I do. Fear of not enough health, money, job security, close relationships—and the list goes on and on. How could I help myself and my clients find greater fearlessness? As I reached back into my *feel-good* memories, I found that each time I connected to the peace I felt when I remembered the angelic voices that saved my life, not once but three times, I realized *I was not alone and never would be.* The sense of that deep relationship has given me enormous strength in times of great challenge.

I searched for other ways to connect to those angelic presences when I wasn't in some type of turmoil, and I found that I could capture that closeness by opening my heart to Mother Nature. Thus, animals became the balm in my life. I have always loved dogs, but not until I was sixty did I find the bond with a horse. I have learned over the last five years how to *join up* with my horses so that we both feel safe and loved. What an extraordinary experience to know that through the language of love, the horse can help you conquer your fears. My first fearless equine teacher was Skye. She has been with me for the last eleven years, and we have grown together in beautiful partnership. Her sweet soul has helped my soul grow in wisdom. Her story is an integral part of this book.

I hope that you will join me on this amazing journey of heart-connectedness to the angelic realm and the world of equine wisdom. Thank you for your curiosity about communication with the non-physical and the soul of a horse that this book represents.

Expect the Extraordinary in YOUR Life!

Introduction

I have faced death three times in my life. I was saved each of those times by a different voice urging me to take specific steps to save myself. Over the last forty years, I have asked myself—why was I saved? Then, in May 2014, I had a very detailed dream. (I rarely remember my dreams.) "Tell your story, tell your story—it will help so many others," the soft voice implored me. I saw myself at a blackboard, and I was teaching a classroom of students about living without fear of death (which is really about living life fully, without so much fear). The classroom had a pink hue all around it, and my spiritual mentor was in the back of the room gently prodding me on with his thoughts of how to help my students get his message. Floating right next to my mentor was a beautiful blue butterfly with wings fluttering so fast I could feel the energy of its excitement even in my dream. That butterfly, on the book cover and in my heart, signifies the art of transformation for each of us.

So, here I am—sharing a message of greater fearless living.

In late 2008, I published my first book, *Bootstraps: A Woman's Guide to Personal Power*, which was my original foray into life as an author. I love writing because at heart, I am a storyteller. When my children were teenagers, I would tell them stories of my fictional friends who were parents of fictional teens who fell into misfortune by not listening to their parents. They still laugh at me today because those stories worked—they stayed out of trouble during those tough growing up years. *Bootstraps* highlights the stories of nine women who picked themselves up by their bootstraps to save their lives from unwanted turmoil, and went on to live in greater personal freedom and joy. Writing this book was a catharsis for me because I had just lost my husband to heart disease, and I wanted other women to know they could recover and recoup from life's challenges.

Expect the Extraordinary is completely different. It delves into the world of dynamic angelic existence. Angels are real! They came to me, not once, but three times to literally save my life. As I look back on these three extraordinary events, I realize that I was supposed to tell these stories so that you, my reader, will know without a doubt that there is more to life than just the physical realm. Why is this so important to me and hopefully, to you? Because when life gets so tough that we want to give up, we won't—because we know we are guided and protected and that we can call upon these magnificent beings to be our lifeline.

The second half of *Expect the Extraordinary* leads us to the story of how I came to know and love horses at the more mature age of sixty-five. My first riding lesson was at sixty—I was the oldest in the class of eight six-year-olds. I loved it! I was scared to death of the horses' size and power, but there was something magical about their eyes. Their eyes were the pathway to their soul, and to mine.

After twenty years, when there were no more angelic life-altering events, I wondered how I could connect again with those angelic guides who saved my life. I meditated, worked with gifted spiritual teachers, and read everything I could get my hands on relating to the spiritual connection of the human to the non-physical world. Then, one day, I visited a barn where a friend of mine worked. I just wandered around the stalls and said "hello" to the horses. One big bay in particular leaned out and whinnied loudly for me

Introduction

to come over. When I reached his stall door, he stuck his head out and sniffed me all over and then snorted. It was as if he were saying, "Why don't you come take me out to play sometime? I may be big, but I love people and you look like fun even if you are a bit of a midget." (I am 5'2" and he was well over 16 hands–BIG.) I was hooked—big time! This started my journey into the spiritual understanding of the world of horses and how angelic presences work with us in our everyday lives, even in the heart of a horse—we just may not realize it or see it at first. Angelic connection comes with faith—what we can't see may still exist—we just have to believe. So, I welcome you to my world of heartbeats and hoofbeats—life is much more than you can see with your eyes. You just have to LIVE FROM YOUR HEART. You just have to BELIEVE!

part one

MY ANGELIC ENCOUNTERS

Arizona Mountains

CHAPTER 1

Whisper 1

Near death on an Arizona mountainside

I'm floating! Where *am* I? What's happening? Why can't I feel anything? From over my right shoulder, I hear, "Move your legs NOW! Move them back and forth to keep the 'fire' from moving up into your belly and your heart. You cannot leave now. You must go back to the children." Where was that voice coming from? Where *was* I?

It is 1972 and I am hiking up to Indian caves in the Huachuca Mountains in southern Arizona with my husband, Jim. We had ridden our motorcycle up the twisting, turning mountain roads and parked it at the base of the small mountain where the caves were located. We struggled to get a foothold on the steep hillside and then, as we finally got inside the cave entrance, a major thunderstorm came out of nowhere. Over the claps of thunder, Jim yelled that he was going back down to start the bike before the rain drenched the starter. As he ran out the cave, he began slipping and sliding down the hill. These torrential rains came often in August; it was the rainy season. But the parched Arizona desert couldn't absorb such a deluge, so the rain just ran like a river down the hillside. Jim turned around after reaching the bottom and frantically motioned for me to come down as quickly as possible. I ran out of the entrance of the cave into rain coming down in sideway sheets. I began slipping and losing my footing. All of a sudden, out of my right eye, I could see a fence (separating the state of Arizona from the military base, Ft. Huachuca) with a metal post, and I thought maybe I could use it to stabilize myself as I fought my way down the steep incline.

Mud! So much mud! It's in my nose, my mouth, my eyes. How did I get on my stomach? I was standing up before. Why don't I have any feeling in my legs? Back and forth, back and forth—didn't someone just tell me to move my legs? I struggled so hard to inch my legs along, but they were like a dead weight. I could feel heat coming into my pelvic area, then into my stomach. I *had* to move, and, *now*. I finally realized that some serious accident had occurred, but there was no pain. I couldn't feel anything. Not even the cold rain. Then, suddenly, I started to sob. Was I going to be OK? Could I get back to my children? The voice, whose was it? It was a soft, but urgent voice telling me to move. I remember now. In the fog of whatever this accident was, I remember seeing my children's faces—Chris on the left (six years old) and Cathy on the right (four years old). I knew I couldn't leave them. Not now, not ever. Then, suddenly, Jim was there lifting me up and carrying me down the hill on his back. I couldn't walk but was getting feeling back in my body—freezing in the pouring rain. My body was shaking so hard. I was going into shock. I yelled into Jim's ear, "What happened?" He yelled back over the thunder, "You got hit by lightning. Your clothes have almost melted off your body. We have to get you dry and warm before your heart goes into greater shock. (Jim was a Major in military Special Forces and knew battlefield first aid.)

Jim got us both on the bike, and held onto my arms around his neck because I couldn't hold on to him on my own. He had seen an old hunter's cabin on our way up the mountain and headed there. We finally got to the cabin. There were two other bikers there trying to get out of the storm as well. They took one look at me and helped Jim carry me inside. Then, the three guys emptied some gas from each bike into an old pot from the cabin and used that to start a fire. I had to strip down to my underwear because the polyester clothes had melted into tattered rags. I had to get warm. The other two bikers were on a weekend trip, so they had additional clothes. They gave me jeans and a shirt.

Jim helped me change into dry clothing. I will be forever grateful to those two guys. How wonderful they were! When someone found an old telephone on the wall, Jim called the operator and got connected to the military hospital at Ft. Huachuca. The ambulance started the trip up the mountainside to the hunter's cabin, but then called back to the cabin phone to tell Jim that, with the rain, the steep incline was almost impossible to climb. My husband told them that I was in serious shock and that he thought my heart was really compromised. Within 15–20 minutes, I could hear the siren. I was so thankful since I was going in and out of consciousness. I just wanted to sleep. Jim and the other two bikers kept me talking. The medics got me on a stretcher with many heated blankets, which I can still feel to this day. How wonderful to be warm! I just remember them telling me over and over again how lucky I was. Then, on to the emergency room where all types of tests were run to see what physical damage I sustained. Again, the doctors kept reiterating how lucky I was to be alive. They had lost two hikers the week before, both conducting lightning strikes through the roots of large trees up through their feet.

After two days in the hospital, I was released. I was twenty-eight years old, and my life had been saved by a voice. Whose voice? From where had it come? And, why the words *fire* and *belly*? I was so naive and so incredibly busy raising my two children that I didn't even try to find out who or what had spoken to me. I just thought it was so weird that I had better keep it to myself. Jim didn't believe me when I told him. He said I was hallucinating, trying to save myself. Maybe he was right.

It would be years before I put together a pattern that was emerging in my life. Now, looking back on that lightning strike of forty years ago, I have come to realize that I am SO very grateful for this wake-up call. I was just beginning to believe in myself as a woman—one who could now be responsible for her own destiny. This life-altering event was leading me onto a deeper path of self-discovery. I was truly blessed!

Human Energy Output

CHAPTER 2

Whisper 2

Divine intervention in New York City

What a beautiful night in New York City! Warm and temps in the low 70s in early October. I was enormously happy. I had a great new job and an even better new relationship. It took a while to get to this point because after the lightning accident several years earlier, I stayed in my marriage to Jim for six more years, knowing that it wasn't working and that I was too afraid to leave. When I finally decided that I could raise Cathy and Chris on my own, the floodgates of employment opportunities opened up to me. I held several jobs in New York City before I finally found my dream job with a marketing company based in New York and Connecticut, and literally headquartered down the street from where I lived in Westport, Connecticut. Wow, synchronicity at it's finest!

My new relationship was with Bob Kipperman, and it would turn into an engagement and a 28-year marriage before he passed away in 2007 from a rare heart disease. But this particular night in New York was magical. We had eaten at a great Italian restaurant, Il Menestrello, and we were strolling up Madison Avenue to the apartment of a friend on Madison and 83rd. The friend graciously offered up his one bedroom condo for us to stay for the weekend. We both had been working so hard and then commuting every night on the train back to Connecticut. Bob worked as a vice president at CBS Television, so he experienced many stressful situations. The weekend getaway was such a treat, just what we needed.

As we strolled up Madison from 50th Street, it would take us about an hour to slowly make our way to 83rd Street. We were kibitzing about my new job and Bob's upcoming trip to a televised golf tournament. We were holding hands, with each of our briefcases being carried by our outside hands as we reached 80th and Madison. Suddenly, a tall man and a short, very nervous younger man came up behind us and said, "Back up against the fence and don't do anything stupid, like try to get attention from the people walking across the street." I was dumbfounded. What was happening? Were these jokers real, and were they robbing us? The next sentence confirmed it. Tall Guy said, "Give me all your jewelry and your money. Where's your wallet, Mr. big shot? Give it to me." Bob was in shock too and said, "Don't take the jewelry; it was a gift." The Tall One just howled with laughter. "OK, I'll send it to my mother for safe keeping." Short Guy was just standing next to Tall Guy, holding the gun, with his arm shaking like a leaf. This must have been his initiation into the world of big-time crime. I started to take off my new necklace (a recent gift from Bob) when Tall Guy just reached over and tore it off my neck. That yank really hurt—the necklace had a thick gold chain on it. I could feel the panic rising up inside of me. These guys were serious offenders.

Suddenly, a voice broke through my terror. In my head, I could hear: "Fall to the ground on your knees. Tell them you are pregnant, and you are going to vomit and be sick all over the sidewalk. Do it now!" The voice was gentle but very firm. It wasn't the same voice that came to me when I was struck by lightning. It was firmer, stronger. I did exactly as I was told. I fell to the sidewalk and yelled, "I am pregnant. I'm going to be sick." Bob almost had a heart attack and said, "Sue, not now!" Tall Guy said, "Get up, Lady, now, or I will blow your head off." I answered, "I can't. I am so sick. You'll have to shoot me."

He was so startled by what I said that he looked around and could see people on the other side of Madison Avenue stopping and staring at us. He finally said, "I don't know if you're really sick, Lady, but we got everything we came for. We are outta here." (Saving face, so important!) Then, they slowly sauntered off laughing as they crossed Madison to Fifth Avenue and The Metropolitan Museum of Art.

Bob was so jacked up and furious that we had been robbed. He took off his suit jacket, handed it to me, and said he was going after them. I couldn't believe it and begged him to call 911 instead. But he took off running and yelled back at me to go to the nearest restaurant and call 911. I ran over to the other side of the street, found a small Greek deli, and asked to use the phone because we had just been robbed. (This was before cell phones, of course.) I finally connected with 911, and they sent police squad cars racing up the wrong way on Fifth Avenue to the Museum.

I ran to the Museum carrying two briefcases and Bob's jacket while three police cars jumped the sidewalk in front of me and took off down the museum sidewalk. They piled out of their squad cars and surrounded the suspects, who gave up immediately with six guns pointed at them and more coming. Bob was ushered back to where I was standing, and then he yelled to the police; "Here's the gun, on the ground by the bushes. Let me have it. I'll kill them!" A little adrenaline speaking up? The gun was retrieved, but nowhere could they find the stolen jewelry.

The police pushed the two suspects into two separate squad cars while they looked for the necklace and Bob's wallet. Suddenly, one of the cops yanked Tall Guy out of the squad car and furiously pulled out the back seat. There, under the back seat cushion was the wallet and the necklace. Now they had all they needed—stolen items and the gun.

We finally got to our friend's condo at about midnight. Bob never went to sleep; he was too keyed up. I, on the other hand, had one glass of wine, and I was out until the phone rang at 6 a.m. It was my babysitter in Connecticut telling us that the Manhattan police were looking for us. She gave us the phone number of the precinct that had called, and Bob called them back. They wanted us to come to Police Headquarters immediately. Something had come up, and they needed identity confirmation of the thieves right away. A squad car was sent to pick us up with the same detective who had overseen the case from the night before. We felt safer knowing that the same guy who captured these crazies would be there for us. They didn't tell us right away what was happening. They just put each of us in separate rooms to question us. They showed us photos of each guy and asked if we recognized either of them. We both firmly confirmed that they were the two guys who held us up. Then, they told us why we had been brought in. Tall Guy had murdered two doormen on the West Side of Manhattan two weeks before, because they didn't have enough money on them to make it worth Tall Guy's time to rob them. We both were stunned. We could have died right there on Madison Avenue at 8:30 on a Friday night. That urgent angelic voice saved us. When Bob asked me later why I dropped to the ground with a gun pointed at my head, I told him about the "whisper." He didn't believe me. I don't know if I believed it, either. But, several years later, when my life was saved again by another voice, I knew someone was trying to give me a message. But, what message? What am I supposed to do with these messages? In 1988, I finally realized these communications were given to me to get my attention, and to share with others how each of us has angelic saviors who want to connect with us. If we believe, they will intervene on our behalf.

CHAPTER 3

Whisper 3

Cancer in Connecticut

It is now 1988, and I am still commuting into New York City to work. That daily grind was truly sapping me of all of my life energy. I abhorred the company I was working for. They abused their employees with fear tactics, never giving a thought to how to motivate people to do their best with positive reinforcement. I had to get out of there! But how? I felt that I was in a deep hole. Bob and I were paying for two homes, three cars, and four kids in college at the same time. I was trapped, and the deep anxiety I was feeling was stifling. These feelings had been stuffed inside of me for over a year, with several years of uneasiness prior to now, and it was all culminating in panic.

It is August 1988, and I am getting dressed to catch the 8:20 a.m. commuter train from Westport, Connecticut, to Grand Central Station in the city. When I came out of the shower, I went to Bob, who was also hurrying to get dressed, and said: "Honey, I have a mosquito bite on my shoulder. Can you take a look at it? It seems to be bleeding, and it is really itchy." Bob looked at it and said, "Sue, that's not a bite, it's something else. It is really dark, and it is bleeding. It looks like a mole that has become infected. You really should go to a doctor and get it checked out." I didn't have any time for doctors right then. I had year end sales numbers to meet and had to get on the road to client meetings in New York. So, I just put a band-aid on it and ran to catch the 8:20 train.

While in New York that Tuesday, I was having my hair colored and cut on my lunch hour. While I was in the salon chair talking to my hairdresser, I said to her: "Gail, do you know the name of a good dermatologist? I have an infected mole and need to get it looked at." She said that not only did she have a name, but he was the president of the American Dermatological Association. His name was Darrel Rigel. I took his name and number and stored it in my address book (still no cell phones yet). I'd call him later in the week, as soon as I found time after getting back to the office.

After lunch that day, I was rushing to my last appointment of the day in lower Manhattan as I passed a building on Madison Avenue and 35th Street. Suddenly, out of the blue, a soft, but firm voice shouted at me. "STOP!" What? Who's there? There's no one on this side of the street but me. Then, the voice came again, "Stop here. Go inside." I looked up at the building on my left, and there was a bronze plaque with the name of the offices: Rigel Dermatology Group, Darrel S. Rigel, MD. I was absolutely dumfounded. Where did this loud whisper come from? This is the same doctor that Gail had mentioned. I felt compelled to go inside and ask at the front desk when I could see Dr. Rigel. Divine guidance was back. But, surely, this had nothing to do with saving my life again.

At the front desk of Dr. Rigel's office, the receptionist said that he didn't have anything available until late September. She then asked what my problem was. I told her that I had a mole that seemed to be infected and was bleeding. She jerked her head up from her calendar and said that the doctor would want to see me right away. How about this coming Thursday? I stuttered that Thursday was OK. I could see that she was concerned. I was then scared. What was the matter with my mole?

Thursday came, and I went back to Rigel's office, so scared that I could barely breathe. Bob thought it was just an infection. Nothing to worry about, but he hadn't seen that nurse's face. As soon as I was in the examining room, Dr. Rigel came in and asked to see my mole. It was on my left shoulder. He looked at it for just a few seconds and then said: "Sue, do you know what melanoma is?" I said no. He then explained that it is a very serious skin cancer, and if this mole was not removed right away, the cancer could spread, and I could die. I couldn't catch my breath. I was in shock! In my mind, I was still at the infection stage. Wow! He then told me I would have to have an immediate biopsy, and the results would be back tomorrow, Friday. He would put a rush on it. They took the biopsy. I struggled to get my blouse back on. Immediately I went to the nearest pay phone to call Bob and tell him I had skin cancer and would need an operation. I canceled my afternoon sales calls and caught a train back home.

Friday came. At 2 p.m. Dr. Rigel himself called. The mole was cancerous and would have to be removed by a plastic surgeon in Manhattan the following Tuesday. Knowing that I was a tennis player and how important that was to me, the doctor said they would do everything they could to save my left shoulder. I couldn't believe my ears. Me, cancer? I took such good care of myself with exercise and diet. I was SO scared. I didn't want to die. I wanted to see my children graduate from high school and college, and have them find great jobs and wonderful spouses. I had to be here for all of those very special passages in life.

The surgery came and went with no complications. Thank God! As I was convalescing at home, being so grateful to be alive and equally grateful that I listened to that voice on Madison Avenue, I realized that I had to leave my job. I had worked in this sales field for over ten years, and I was bored stiff and really could not tolerate the company management. They manipulated their employees with threats of job loss or loss of sales accounts regardless of how much revenue we brought into the coffers. How was I going to disentangle myself from this high-paying job? How was I going to tell my husband that we had to downsize, and not just a little but a lot?

I remember the conversation with Bob as clearly as if it were yesterday. I told him I couldn't keep working at this job, that I wouldn't take a chance of being miserable any longer and literally making myself ill so that we could keep a second home and all of the other goodies. He was shocked, but understanding of the situation. We sold a car and a house, and I gave my resignation the next month. I felt free but scared. What would I do with myself? I decided to go after a path that made a difference and made me feel good about myself.

I took six months off to explore my options. All of the kids were finally getting out of college, so downsizing was easier than we had thought. When I at last came up for air, a friend told me that I should contact The Stillpoint Institute in New Hampshire because mind/body research was something I loved. I called Meredith Young-Sowers, the founder of the Institute, and was so excited about the curriculum they had to offer that I enrolled immediately. Meredith teaches her students to interpret the messages the body sends through its organs and bodily systems, as well as through illnesses. I love this work and still today help my clients through life-changing times using the physical/emotional/spiritual model I learned.

During the second Stillpoint module the class was learning what the different cancers were messaging. When we came to the skin cancer section (melanoma), I was shocked—the toxicity of an environment in which you find yourself can cause anger at oneself for not making the needed changes to leave those negative circumstances, and that anger can manifest itself on the skin, from the inside out. So, now I knew that my thoughts were responsible for my continued unhappiness of seven years regarding my previous job. If I kept up that negativity, I could cause another illness. I have been using this Stillpoint model for twenty years, and not once has it been anything but right on target, regardless of the illness or organ of the body. Our bodies speak to us. They want us to live in joy (balance) and not just live our lives for the security and happiness of others. Our bodies are our earthly message centers!

part two

OTHERS' LIFE SAVING STORIES

Scott Gearen several years after his accident
(Courtesy of Scott Gearen)

CHAPTER 4

Scott's near-death experience

When I met John Pighini, my husband, in late 2008, he had read *Bootstraps* and asked me about my lightning near-death experience (NDE). He was very interested because one of his closest friends, Scott, also had an NDE in a parachute jump accident, and he had other similar spiritual occurrences to mine. Scott and I sat down in December 2014, and he relayed to me his unbelievable history. I will do my best to paraphrase his story.

On February 4, 1987, Scott Gearen, an Air Force Pararescueman, was making his 90th free-fall parachute jump out of a Marine CH-46 helicopter flying 13,000 feet above the cold, frozen fields of Virginia. Scott was on temporary training duty, attached to a Navy Seal team stationed at Virginia Beach, Virginia. Air Force Pararescuemen (PJs) are an elite air, sea, and ground force who are "personnel recovery specialists, trained in emergency medicine and combat tactics to execute the most extreme rescue missions across the globe" (USAF Pararescue, 2015). Scott, an Air Force Master Sergeant, was part of a team conducting a routine training free-fall jump. In a free-fall jump the parachutist falls through the sky with a predetermined parachute opening closer to the ground than is usual. Scott had made similar test jumps many times before.

As planned, Scott plunged 9,500 feet through the silver-blue sky before pulling his ripcord to open his chute at 3,500 feet. Just as he was checking his canopy to make sure it had opened fully, Scott's life came to an abrupt standstill. A fellow jumper, still in free-fall, traveling straight down at approximately 120 mph, realized that he was going to plow into Scott. The jumper above Scott instinctively pulled himself into "cannonball" position to protect himself from the collision. Plowing through Scott's open canopy, the free-faller's impact destroyed and ripped apart five of the seven nylon cords that held Scott's parachute upright and, at the same time, knocked Scott unconscious. Scott was now a human missile, plunging uncontrollably to the ground below. His body, with torn parachute trailing behind him, fell more than 3,000 feet, impacting the ground at approximately 90 mph. None of the other men still in free-fall or on the ground could do anything but watch in horror as Scott fell to the icy terrain below.

Scott Gearen hit the ground like a speeding bullet while two other Seals on the same jump, and still under canopy, followed him to the ground and landed as close as possible to him. They found Scott lying face down, not moving, and in a pool of blood—they thought he was dead. Another Pararescueman arrived on the scene shortly thereafter to administer critical support, and they soon realized, to their disbelief and amazement, that Scott was still alive. He was unconscious and seriously injured, needing immediate life-saving medical attention. He was airlifted almost an hour later to Portsmouth Navy Hospital with life threatening injuries, including an open skull fracture and crushed larynx, nose, cheekbones, and eye sockets. Scott's excellent physical conditioning, due to his cardio fitness and weight lifting, was a major factor contributing to his survival.

Scott does not remember the accident at all, neither the airborne collision nor hitting the ground. What he does remember is the euphoric feeling he felt when a male-like voice came to him and said, "It's time to go." Scott said back to the male voice, "I'm not ready to go now." He could immediately feel what was happening to him. He was surrounded by a softening light over his right shoulder where three silhouetted figures were beckoning him. He was not in pain but rather at total peace and completely blissful. He knew his consciousness was very alive, but he was no longer constrained by his body.

When Scott said, "I'm not ready to go now," he came back into his body and found himself in the intensive care unit at the hospital. It took him a year and a half of time in and out of the hospital dealing with multiple surgeries to be recovered enough to reapply for his job as a Pararescueman. Scott was able to requalify for his job and went on to complete over 500 more free-fall parachute jumps before he was forced to retire due to an accumulation of injuries.

Today, June 2015, Scott is still bravely dealing with the aftermath of that calamitous fall. He protects his health at all costs and is profoundly grateful to be alive to share his story.

While comatose, Scott connected with the angelic realm. He was telepathically given insightful teachings that he remembers word for word. He wants to share the messages he received with others, so that all who listen can anchor these insights inside of themselves.

- God is real! Who can prove that God is real? No one; but Scott says that his travels to the *light* prove to him that God is very real and "provided me the experience and the proof that I needed to know without a doubt that God is real and so is life after death."

- Scott had a normal Christian child's upbringing, but he had the same scary feelings about dying that all children feel as they are growing up. His mother was very instrumental in helping him deal with those lonely feelings of death. As he grew a little older, he felt he had unusual intuitive feelings. He remembers wanting a pony more than anything else in the world. He prayed hard every day for a week, and he just knew he was going to get a pony. Soon thereafter, he went to the local rodeo with his family and put his name in a box for the drawing for a young horse. He was so excited to be there, and you know what? He won that pony. He knew God was real even as a child.

As an adult, Scott notes what he learned from his tragic accident: "The NDE I had was not an accident. It was an event, a significant event for me to learn from. Its purpose was for me to reconnect with my intuitive self again, to know God is real, and to share my experience with others. Possibly, someone with the same feelings I had as a small child—afraid of dying—can find comfort in my sharing with them my experience with God. When life on this earth is over, the soul will go on. I truly believe that. I was given a second chance to continue to live my life here on earth and to share this experience with others. God is real, and so is life after death."

So, taking our cue from Scott's words, let me summarize with the following thoughts.

- What is your purpose here on earth? Hopefully, you can say it is to be the best you can be in all aspects of life.

- Live life fully! Take chances to feel who you truly are. Find your freedom!

- Learn to listen to your heightened self—your intuitive self. It lives in your heart and that is where the angels can reach you.

- The angelic realm is always with you.

- Love learning about all of life. Educate yourself daily.

- Life is not over on the physical plane; it continues on after you die.

- You make your life what it is. You do have control of the final outcome of events affecting you by how you perceive the end result. What do you learn from each of the experiences in your life?

Scott's near-death experience

- You are in charge of your life. Your choices will lead you to your destinations in life. Choose wisely!
- Don't worry about things you cannot control. "Don't sweat the small stuff, and it's all small stuff."
- Be more aware of your time here on earth—life is a gift. Be productive.
- Appreciate all of what you see in nature—animals, flowers, the sky—all of it.
- *Never quit! Never, ever give up!*

As Scott says, "When faced with a choice of life or death, choose life! Surviving the accident was mostly out of my control due to the injuries I sustained. However, my will to survive was still in my control. God gave me another opportunity at life to share my story with you. I am so blessed!"

Never quit! Never, ever give up!

Scott in his parachute after his accident

Donnie Yance
(Courtesy of Donald Yance)

CHAPTER 5

Donnie's conversation with God

I've known Donald Yance for 30 years. He is my go-to guy for all of my natural health guidance and was one of the first alternative health practitioners I met who truly treated his patients holistically. He is intensely interested in all of you—your physical self, your emotional self, and your spiritual self. Donnie studied to be a Franciscan monk but left the monastery when he felt a calling to help others heal on both a physical and spiritual level. He is a master herbalist and certified nutritionist as well as a Secular Franciscan, SFO.

When I met Donnie in 1985, he was the supplement guru at a local health food store in Westport, Connecticut. The line to reach him at the counter to learn from his expert advice was always down around two separate aisles in the store. The store finally instituted an appointment-only protocol so that other patrons could more easily shop in the store. From the tiny natural food store in Westport to opening his own office in Norwalk, Connecticut, and then moving to Ashland, Oregon, to found an all-encompassing alternative health center is the story of someone passionately following his dream and having that dream manifest itself on a larger scale over and over again.

Donnie's dream of being able to help as many people as possible has led him to be in high demand at major hospitals and oncology centers in the United States. He has become one of the most sought after speakers and consultants on herbal medicine and alternative healing. He is a truly gifted healer and a wonderful friend.

When I had my most recent phone consultation with Donnie (he in Oregon, me in Virginia) in May 2015, I casually asked how he was, and he told me that he had almost died. I couldn't believe what he was saying. Here is a man who is the epitome of health, living a balanced life of work, play, and spirituality with a client calendar booked out a year in advance. What happened? I was shell-shocked to say the least. Here is a capsule summary of Donald Yance's amazing story relayed to me the day of my May phone consult.

- Good Friday, April 3, 2015: Donnie woke up feeling flushed, fatigued, and feverish. He couldn't eat and went home after some appointments in the morning to take natural flu supplements and get some rest. He felt nauseated and was urinating every five to ten minutes. His headache was monstrous.

- April 4 and 5: No relief from the flu symptoms, and by the evening of the 5th he was having neurological and adrenal issues.

- Monday, April 6: Blood in his urine, and still no sleep or food.

- Tuesday morning, April 7: The fever was down, but he was still urinating every five to ten minutes, and his head felt fuzzy. He decided to go to the local emergency room, although he hadn't been to any hospital in many, many years. The doctors there determined, through blood work, that he had a medium grade bladder infection. He came home from the ER but still had a very rough night. He felt a great loss of salt, particularly in his brain. He knew he was in a life-threatening situation.

- Wednesday, April 8: His tongue had swelled up and turned black and furry. Again, no sleep, and he had a distinct electrical feeling in his body. Suddenly, his journey became one of *out* of his body versus *in* his body. Donnie felt he was being pulled into a vortex of energy, still experiencing great pain but feeling tremendous joy and love at a the same time. He slid into the energy of an elephant, which he feels is the most spiritual animal on the planet (with the horse coming in a close second). While in the vortex with the elephant, he encountered Christ, the energy of all love and joy.

- Thursday, April 9: Donnie went back to the ER, as the infection had gotten worse. He was having a serious reaction to the antibiotics the doctors had given him, and his furry tongue had become worse. He went home and began vigorously dosing on natural supplements, using high dosage compounded formulas from his clinic, The Mederi Center for Natural Healing. He discontinued the antibiotic. He was sleeping off and on, and trying to eat some.

- Friday, April 10 and Saturday, April 11: Donnie was starting to feel a little better, but he was still very fuzzy in his brain and had a huge craving for salt and watermelon, which he later credits to saving his life along with all of the supplementation. He consumed copious amounts of nerve enhancing natural remedies. His nervous system was highly compromised because of the illness, but also because he had been moving in and out of a universal energy vortex with the elephant as his guide.

- Sunday, April 12 and Monday, April 13: Donnie was definitely feeling better but still had neurological and stomach issues to heal. The urinary tract infection was almost gone, but he was very weak.

When I asked Donnie if he would be willing to share his story with you, my reading audience, he didn't hesitate to let me bring this amazing journey to you. His hope, and mine too, is that his story will help you know that you are not alone when life gets very challenging.

I asked Donnie what he thought caused this sudden onset of kidney and bladder issues. Before hearing his answer, you need to know that Donnie is a prolific writer of alternative health research books that promote the use of adaptogenic herbs and cancer healing supplementation. He lectures all over the country on healing and nutrition. So, what could cause this sudden turnaround in this man's health? He told me that he was not listening to his intuitive guidance about when to slow down, when to take a break and let his body relax. He would work for long hours at a time, never leaving his office, and often forgetting to eat or visit the restroom. When you are so dedicated to helping your patients and the world at large, you sometimes lose yourself in the process. That is what happened to Donnie. He lost his way in the digital world of research, doing everything he could to find answers to help his patients heal.

I asked Donnie what he would like the readers of *Expect the Extraordinary* to learn from his experiences. He gave me these words to give to you:

- "God is most impressed with humility.

- Live from your heart.

- Seek beauty, truth, and love.

- Fresh bread is the most important nourishing food of all because it binds us together. Bread provides more than physical sustenance. We use the phrase 'breaking bread together' to indicate the sharing of a meal with someone. In a spiritual and social sense, bread binds us together in our humanity and offers a sense of community. 'For we many are one bread, and one body: for we are all partakers of that one bread' (1 Corinthians 10:17). In the Jewish Passover meal, bread plays an integral role. The Jews were to eat unleavened bread during the Passover feast and then for seven days following as a celebration of the exodus from Egypt. God rained down 'bread from heaven' to sustain the nation (Exodus 16:4), referring to it as 'manna' (Exodus 16:31). There are many reasons to appreciate a humble loaf of good bread. Everyone, no matter what his or her economic status, can afford to make bread. You need not be wealthy to afford bread—God made bread for both the rich and the poor. Organic wheat and other whole grains used to make bread are inexpensive, yet nutritious, ingredients. Whole grains, including wheat, and specifically heirloom wheat, have the least negative impact on the environment. And last, but certainly not least, modern scientific research has validated the enormous health benefits of whole grains.

- Use technology sparingly. You can lose your heart-centered focus to the outside physical world if you live in technology too much of your day.

- Botanical medicine saved my life. The wisdom acquired from ancient and traditional medicine must come first. The knowledge acquired from modern medicine and research must come second, and never the other way around.

- The physical and the spiritual in all of us must be co-partners in inspiring us to live lives of great joy and passion.

- Death is fearful for most, and we need to prepare ourselves as if today is our last day. Live life fully each day!"

Donnie continues, "Through my illness came an experience I can only describe as spiritual rapture, where I endured many days of unremitting suffering, and simultaneously unparalleled love and joy. From a place of raw vulnerability, deep love, and humility, I learned a great many truths and discovered renewed strength, courage, and wisdom. Through this learning, one of the gifts bestowed upon me was the conception of a special blend of sacred essential oils for the purpose of anointment. This formulation came to me from both my deep intuitive wisdom of medicine and my connection to the Divine, as I was recovering from my own illness, searching for remedies, and reflecting on my roots as a Franciscan monk. My sacred blend includes frankincense, lavender, Holy basil, rose, nutmeg, myrrh, and sandalwood.

"I created the Oil of Anointment as a means to simply assist people in drawing closer to their spiritual essence, or seeking spiritual enlightenment, and especially for the sick, suffering, and those who are ascending (dying), since I often work with people who are terminally ill and seeking peace and connection to God. When we anoint and perform unction, we are calling upon divine influence, a holy emanation, spirit, and the power of God. Unction not only unites us to Spirit, but creates in us renewed Spirit, an inner sanctuary.

"These human, energetic "bubbles" we call bodies are a gift. I have so often abused mine and taken it for granted. It can only do so much. Your body is the house that your soul lives in. It must be cherished and treated with divine respect, yet we must surrender our body at some point and we cannot be afraid.

"I have found this to be a fundamental truth in my work with patients, their families, and with the medical profession. Fear is a natural and understandable reaction to illness; none of us wants to be sick, and few of us are prepared to deal with the many unknowns that come with the diagnosis of a serious illness.

"I believe the answer is to make peace with the state of unknowing. When we learn how to be fully alive in this moment—accepting that we don't know what the next moment may bring—we free ourselves to live a life that is richer and more fulfilling than any life lived by the strictures of control. What is most important is the willingness to embrace the unknown, what Christian mystics call the 'cloud of unknowing.'

"As a practicing secular Franciscan, I find great solace in my practice of daily prayer. But I do not pray with the intent of petitioning God. When we make requests of God, we are attempting to control outcome, which merely leads us back to fear when our problems are not solved in the way that we think they should be. We have no control over God, and we cannot know or understand God with words. The only way that we can know God is through love. We must relinquish the practice of petitioning God to answer our prayers. Instead, we must let go and trust. We must pray with pure love, because it is only with our hearts that we can penetrate the cloud of unknowing. We must cultivate a place of inner peace, quiet our minds, and allow pure love to connect us to God. We must forget everything, and in this forgetting, we discover that God is everywhere, and that we are everywhere as well. We become more comfortable with uncertainty, and thus are better able to fully inhabit the present moment. We must recognize with humility that uncertainty is inherent in all situations, and we should be open to the ever-present possibility of the surprising, the mysterious, and most of all the holy.

"'Entering into the mystery,' Pope Francis explains, 'means the ability to wonder, to contemplate; the ability to listen to the silence and to hear the tiny whisper amid great silence by which God speaks to us' . . . it 'demands that we not be afraid of reality: that we not be locked into ourselves, that we not flee from what we fail to understand, that we not close our eyes to problems or deny them, that we not dismiss our questions' . . . 'To enter into the mystery means going beyond our own comfort zone, beyond the laziness and indifference which hold us back, and going out in search of truth, beauty, and love.'

"I pray that this open and candid sharing of my experience, as well as my personal faith with God, inspires you onward to explore greater mystical heights through your own relationship with the Divine and lights under you a renewed passion to love more."

part three

FINALLY FOUND IT . . .

A FORMULA FOR GREATER FEARLESS LIVING

CHAPTER 6

Journey from corporate America to spiritual seeker

From 1972 to 1988, sixteen years is what it took for me to believe in my own feelings about what happened, not allowing others to discount my experiences just because they were afraid of the reality of what was happening. After being struck by lightning, mugged in New York, and diagnosed with cancer, I was being forced by the universe, if you will, to get on a path other than just *existing* in the physical world and living my life through someone else's eyes. Now, in 2015, forty-three years later, I am *finally* recognizing the gift of these angelic connections, not just because my life was saved, but because I realize it was saved for a purpose. That purpose is to write, teach, and speak of a world larger than what we see each day. To let you, the reader, know that a life of greater meaning and happiness is possible if you *believe* that you are never alone. You can live fearlessly knowing that there is love and support for each new step you take.

From the lightning strike to the cancer scare, what did I learn? I discovered that no one needs a near-death experience, being held up at gunpoint, or cancer to listen to the guidance of his or her intuitive self and angelic guides. They come to us each day in the form of little taps on the shoulders to give us answers. It may be by way of a magazine or newspaper article, something we see on a website, a friend or family member's comment, a TV show or movie, or a conversation with a coworker. All of these "subtle angelic suggestions," as well as your connection to Mother Nature, will tickle your intuition, which is where all of your answers lie to the questions you may have. *Your intuitive life lives in your heart.* Just ask yourself a question, and your intuition will be there for you with the exact right answer. *Do not use your head, use your heart.* Your heart has a brain of its own. I put my right hand (I am right hand dominant) over my heart to silently get the answers I am seeking. Then, I put the same hand next to the side of my head to see what answer comes from there. Try it! See what you find.

In the next chapters, we will look at how we can find greater personal freedom in our lives. Just remember, "Your life is too precious a gift to allow its path to depend on the approval of others." (from *Bootstraps: A Woman's Guide to Personal Power* by Sue Kipperman)

CHAPTER 7

How my life changed and how yours can too

For more than forty years I was a spiritual seeker. I still am today. I took every course I could find that would put me in touch with my intuitive self and the angelic realm that had guided me. I so wanted to connect again, and this time without life-threatening events to call angelic guides into my realm. But I guess they had decided it was time for me to be on my own.

So, in the ensuing years, I left my corporate world behind and sought out a career in alternative health and spirituality. It felt so good to do something that really resonated with my being, not what society thought I should be doing. I learned so much as a corporate executive, but it was a struggle sometimes to find the *fire* in the more materialistic world. I searched and searched for arenas that really pinged my heart. I became a certified hypnotherapist, a hands-on energy healer (the lightning event helped with that—I still have electricity in my body today), an advanced intuitive energy healer, and, today, I practice full-time as a life transition coach. My deep desire is to help others find their soul's desire. We all are born with gifts and talents that want to be fulfilled. What are yours? How do you find them and put them to work for you?

Most people with whom I have worked over the past twenty years are more afraid of living and taking chances than of actually dying. I know I am still afraid of doing certain things to this day, including speaking in front of large groups, riding my horse at a fast gait, or writing this book. What if I fail? I live in a comfort zone that keeps me safe, but bored. So, I work very hard each day to check in with my heart—"What do I feel about what I am doing RIGHT now? Is it giving me joy or is it just helping pass the time of day?" Just passing time is awful! Am I just waiting to grow old and die?

I've been there, on the brink of death. I have to remind myself to do only those things that bring me joy and excite me. Does that mean I don't do the dishes that are piling up in the sink? No, it doesn't, because the mess I will have to clean up later brings me greater angst. Cleaning up now *does* bring me joy, because it brings the order to my life that I want, helping me create my future of greater excitement. In the next chapter we will discuss how your cells crave that excitement and expansion. I use the term *excitement* because excitement to me is anything that lights the fire within me. Whether I might be learning Japanese or learning to play the guitar, I can feel excitement bubble up inside me, and I feel more energetic. That's a Path of Passion[sm]. (Path of Passion is the parent company of Livin' the Dream Media and Ranch.)

I want to invite every person into my life and include every experience that helps me get into "the zone" of high passion living. I look for signs every day of messages from my body that tell me I am on the right track. Do I feel energized? Do I feel centered and grounded with no negative feelings? Then, I am on the right track of exploration. Does this person, this book, this interview on TV, or this movie have a message for me? Do I resonate with what is presented to me? If the answer *feels* like a yes, I delve into finding out more about the opportunity to learn that has been given to me. You can do all of these things. They just take being *aware* and having the *intention* to connect more deeply with *yourself*. All of your answers lie within. People, books, TV interviews, movies, etc. are just catalysts for you to go more deeply into your heart to find your answers. They are guideposts from the universe.

After the three life-saving events I experienced, I finally came away with the profound message that when my time came to cross over the rainbow bridge, I didn't want to ever say to myself, "I wish I had...." I so hope that you, my reader, also want to live your life to its fullest.

Let's explore how we get on that Path of Passion[sm]. In the chapters that follow, I will show you what my forty-three years of life research have given me—greater personal freedom.

I'll meet you in the next chapter, "Tool 1: Positivity."

CHAPTER 8

TOOL 1

Positivity—How healthy are your cells?

Positivity—what is it? Why would I want it? Would it make a difference in my life? Positivity, seeing the glass as half full versus half empty, is a *choice* one makes in life. It is a learned behavior that emanates from your heart. Positivity allows your heart rate to beat at an even rhythm, and it puts you into a life-enhancing mode of appreciation, which, in turn, brings more wonderful positive experiences into your life (HeartMath Institute, *Applied Appreciation Research*, heartmath.com).

I have studied much of the ground-breaking research from the HeartMath Institute, founded in 1991 by researcher Doc Childre, to explore how one's heart and brain work together. His life's goal has been to help others see and learn that the heart is at the core of all connections in life. Your heart governs your happiness, your relief of stress, your relationships, and your appreciation of your world. In HeartMath's dynamic e-book, *Applied Appreciation,* we learn that one's heart has a brain of its own, its own intelligence. When you breathe from your heart space, you will find you are calmer, have greater energy. As you do so, a change can occur in your emotional perspective, from fear and worry to peace and gratitude. This takes practice.

Here is an outline of how I have learned to practice gratitude and appreciation.

- I find a quiet place and sit down and close my eyes.
- I focus on my heart.
- I breathe in through my nose and hold that breath for about two seconds. The space at the top of the breath is known as the stillpoint.
- I then breathe out through my mouth.
- I do this several times until I can feel a calming emotion and a quiet happiness overtaking my original feeling.
- You do not have to be sitting in a quiet place. If you are in a tough situation and need to change your fear/anger factor, you can stop right there and concentrate on taking three in and out breaths to help you relax. Look for and find what you can learn from the difficult exchange you are in. You are then able to change your heightened alert response to one of calm interaction. There is always an appreciation factor in any situation you are in. What are you learning? By being in a calmer, appreciative state, you are negating the emotional charge of the difficult situation.

As you practice this technique, you will grow in *appreciation* and *gratitude*. Remember that appreciation is to find the worth or value in something or someone, and gratitude is to be thankful that you found that appreciated something or someone.

HeathMath tells us that when we appreciate the enormous power of our heart's innate ability to guide us, we become more relaxed and less stressed. Your intuition lives in your heart, so as you appreciate your own life more each day, your intuition grows and grows to help you make authentic decisions for yourself. As you become more appreciative and more intuitive, others around you will feel your positive energy, and their lives may change as well. It's the ripple effect of positivity that the universe so wants us to find and spread, like sowing summer seeds.

In chapter 10, we will discuss the Law of Attraction, which is one of twelve universal laws I use to guide myself on my Path of Passion (see more in *Bootstraps: A Woman's Guide to Personal Power*). The Law of Attraction is one of the more than 120 universal laws that has been handed down through centuries. It states that what you think, you will receive. You and I are magnetic beings. We attract those things and feelings that mirror our thoughts.

If I get up grouchy and negative in the morning, I will attract negative experiences in my day. I combat the negative feelings with this simple exercise. When I wake up in the morning, I just stay in bed for a few minutes and allow myself to *feel* a sense of appreciation for all the great things in my life that are here now and the wonderful things I desire that are coming my way. I do this for *17 seconds*, and when I capture those 17 seconds back to back to build to 68 seconds every day, those positive 17 second intervals build on each other and my life starts to become full of positive thoughts and experiences. (A helpful resource here is the Abraham-Hicks CDs, *Co-Creating at Its Best*.) *Seventeen seconds* out of your day to change your life is so little time to take from your schedule in order to grant your heart a path to helping you become happier and much more fulfilled. As you do this, the first key to success is to think *only* about the positive outcome you desire for those *17 seconds*. The second key is to not let anyone get in the way of a tremendous change in the way you choose to live your life with positive thoughts and experiences. Good luck! Amazing what those angels teach us!

Epigenetics

In my first book, *Bootstraps: A Woman's Guide to Personal Power*, I highlighted the work of Dr. Bruce Lipton, an international expert on the scientific cell research called "epigenetics." Epigenetics is the study of how the life we each lead affects and regulates our genes. He calls this science the New Biology—the concept that our bodies respond to our thoughts and emotions, not just to parental programming and genetic origin. To help you understand epigenetics and Dr. Lipton's work, I am now providing an extended quote directly from *Bootstraps: A Woman's Guide to Personal Power*. This helps explain how important it is to realize that we are each totally responsible for how our lives go forward after childhood.

"Dr. Lipton urges us to stop blaming our parents and our childhood experiences for the circumstances of our adult lives. Parents and childhood experiences are not responsible for our actions as adults. We are. No matter how difficult our lives might have been as children, when we reach young adulthood and beyond, we know that we have better choices to make. But often we are so angry at our childhood circumstances that we just want someone to pay for that sorrow. What really happens is that we ultimately take it out on ourselves, not our parental figures. We re-create our own adult reality from the residue of childhood. If you change your thinking, you change your reality.

"On a physical note, just because one of our parents had cancer or heart disease does not mean that we are programmed to have the same disease. There are single-cell disorders like Huntington's disease or cystic fibrosis that can be blamed on one faulty gene, but that situation is found in only 2 percent of the population. Dr. Lipton tells us not to program our bodies for disease with our thoughts of what "might happen" because someone in our family had a particular illness. Our cells have cell receptors that act just like computer chips, storing information. These receptors are affected by our thoughts. Whatever information is fed into our bodies as our "computers" will affect how each of these receptors operates. We create our lives with stored data in our minds. Again we see the Law of Attraction at work—what you think is what you attract to you. Do you feel a lack of financial security? A lack of close relationships? A lack of good health? Or do you feel blessed even if you do not have everything that might make you comfortable? Are you grateful each day just to be alive? Are you grateful that you have a home or a secure place to go to? Are there people in your life who love and care about you? What are you attracting to you?

"Dr. Lipton highlights Einstein's Theory of Relativity because it states that the universe and its inhabitants are all relative to one another. We are not separate: We are all part of the whole. Our physical bodies are vibrating energy, and we live in environments that affect us with vibrating energy, such as the thoughts and feelings of others. What type of environment are you living in? Are those around you vibrating at the same frequency that you are? Is it healthy and uplifting? If not, do not stay in that energy. How do you change your vibration if it isn't working for you? You need to change the vibrational frequency from low to high. You need to change your perception of how you see your life. But what is perception? It is how you understand the circumstances of how you live. Are you living in the real truth of what makes you happy? Is the glass half-full or half-empty? One of the best ways to change your vibration is to change your perception of how you are living your life. Are your activities life-enhancing and fun, or are they "I have to do them?" Do you feel drained of energy or full of pep when you think of your day? *Change* is the magic word. *Change* your thought process and you *change* your actions. Then, the outcome of your life *changes*.

"Gratitude helps us change our perception from "have-not" to "have." Always think about how lucky you are to be where you are in your life. Being grateful can change the vibration that resonates inside of you. You therefore change the experiences that come to you because you are at a higher level of positive vibration. Always ask your heart what is best for you. The heart knows—it has a brain of its own. Bruce Lipton's experiments with cells and their membranes show that the cell's brain (the membrane) can actually be programmed to do as we wish by our thinking of a different path of living. The cell responds by being enhanced with greater life energy just because you changed your thought patterns. This change in thought patterns is free will—the basis of human existence. You have a choice. You can reprogram your life by listening very closely to your thoughts every day to see what you are really thinking, and then *choose* a different thought pattern. Your beliefs become your biology. Your thoughts are the basis of the Law of Attraction in action. This law will tell you exactly, without fail, what you are attracting into your life. What are you thinking about most of the time? The more you think about a desired object or outcome, the more you will vibrate at the rate of attraction needed to manifest your desire: That is what you will draw to you. Your thoughts are the doorway to a great life or a not-so-great life. I encourage my clients and students to journal every day about what they want the next day to look like. The other key is not to be wedded to the outcome of the desired *change* because you don't know what other opportunities of equal greatness might be waiting around the corner. Stay flexible but resilient and feel the energy of success. The excitement of life is always about the journey, not the destination or result.

"Your feelings and emotions will give you the feedback as to what you are attracting into your life. If you are upbeat and excited, you must be on the right track. If not, then *change* your thought in order to *change* your actions and, therefore, your environment. You always have choices."

So, think about this: every time you think a positive thought that enhances who you are, the outer membrane of your cells soaks up that warm, positive energy and duplicates that positive cell again, and again, and again. As a result, your body absolutely vibrates with happiness and joy because *all* of life is fascinating and magical to you. And, this, my friend, is where the angels live—in the positive vibration of your life waiting to partner with you for a thrilling ride!

CHAPTER 9

TOOL 2

Ten Sacred Insights

In 2006 I was right smack in the middle of writing *Bootstraps: A Woman's Guide to Personal Power*. I kept pen and paper everywhere in the house because I remembered when reading an article on the life of J.K. Rowling, dynamic author of The Harry Potter Series, that she had notes everywhere about characters she was birthing and wanted to be sure to get down all the minute details on paper. I thought if J.K. Rowling was writing in this manner, I could surely do the same. So, pen and paper were everywhere: the bedroom, my office, of course, and even the bathroom. I was in the shower early one morning when an overwhelming feeling came to me to get out of the shower and write down some thoughts.

From that very dripping instant, the life of "Ten Sacred Insights to Personal Freedom" was born. As it turned out, each of the ten life teachings started with a "C." They just tumbled out of my subconscious mind at that moment. I didn't even realize what I had written until I picked up the paper and reread what I had scribbled.

Now I want to share the Ten Sacred Insights with you (a review if you have already read *Bootstraps)*. They have been my guideposts when I am reaching for a clearer, more positive thought on how I want to live my life. Being attuned to these insights will allow you to understand why you are here and how you could go forward on your path to personal freedom. When you embody the Ten Sacred Insights, they become your Ten Sacred Attributes that live in your cells and thrive when you nurture them. This process will unite you to aspects of yourself that you may not know very well—your deeper, more expansive spirit.

Ten Sacred Insights on the Path to Personal Freedom
1. **Connection**: Whether we live in Uganda or Utah, we are all connected because we all come from the same divine source. Like mirrors, we reflect our knowledge and learning to one another. Being from the same divine source allows us to connect energetically to each other (feeling someone's pain or happiness). In addition, we can connect to that greater part of who we are, our deep inner self, our spirit. The inner self is the most magnificent part of being human. It is our unique guidance system, where our unconditional love and wisdom reside.

Listen to and work to understand those with whom you interact. Connect to them from the energy of your heart, not your head. Believe that you are part of a world—both physical and nonphysical—that guides and encourages you each moment of every day.

2. **Compassion**: You are perfect, just as you are. You are not here to judge yourself. No matter where you are in your life, you are in a learning mode. Learning about who you are and who you can become is your life's task. When you love and have compassion for yourself, you can then love and honor others. But love yourself first. You are very important to this universe. Spend time nurturing yourself, doing things that excite and light you up—all stimulating self-love.

3. **Creation**: What is your purpose in this lifetime? Find it! When you do, you'll find your passion. It is your responsibility, not someone else's, to create your happiness. Your creation energy is the

example for others to re-create their lives. Your light shines in your passion and power. Creation energy is the expansion of the world. Create the life you truly desire by being involved in the things you love: Take courses and classes, read books and magazines, and investigate any opportunity that excites you. If you have created a life that is not what you want, allow the Law of Transformation to operate, which says that any negative focus in life can be changed when positive intention is put into action.

4. **Communication**: Where is your voice? Speak your deepest desires—not from your head but from your heart. Speak with loving assertion. Your voice counts. Do not be afraid of personal declaration; let the world know who you really are and from what your deepest dreams are made. Only when people lift up their voices will change occur, both in a personal and a global way.

5. **Change**: Life is like the changing of nature's leaves, always discarding the old and anticipating the arrival of the new. We are just like those leaves, just like nature—discarding careers, locations, and relationships that we no longer need, and eagerly awaiting the next season of our personal growth. Do not be afraid of change! Be fearless. Invite change into your life; it keeps you young and vital forever. Make a list of all of those things that you want to look back on and say, "Wow! I am thrilled to have done that!" This list, your Bucket List, is all about how you desire to change your world and the world around you. Joy is the operative word.

6. **Choice**: You have choices. We often think that our choices and options are limited. But they aren't. Maybe we just don't want to make the difficult decision to change direction in life in order to accommodate those choices. We are often afraid of the outcome. Know that fear resides only in the future. It does not live in the present moment. Acknowledge your free will. Often the difference between those who have achieved great success in life and those

who *want* great success is that the highly successful believe they are in charge of how their life proceeds. They believe that they have ultimate free will to live exactly as they please, and they do not care whether their desires to live their dreams are appreciated by others.

7. **Charity**: We are all connected. The disheveled bag lady or homeless veteran begging on the sidewalk comes from the same source we all do. The homeless children in an orphanage come from the same source as you and I. The beaten and abused women in America, Afghanistan, Africa, or Asia come from the same source as you and me. The act of helping save that someone opens your own heart as well. When we realize that we are all connected, our heart energy expands and we get closer to knowing that most magnificent part of who we truly are—our inner, soul-self. Open your heart a little more each day to include others who might otherwise not be in your life. When you step outside yourself to help another, more of that same loving energy comes back to you because you are living in positive action. When you take care of someone else, the universe takes care of you.

8. **Courage**: It takes courage to implement each of these Ten Sacred Insights. It is our ability to free ourselves from the old restraints of peer pressure or family background that transforms courage into the celestial key that unlocks the doors to our dreams. Take one new step each day toward living fearlessly. Do something different each day: Drive to work using a new route, or tell someone close to you exactly how you feel about a topic that is very personal to you. Don't play the "what if" game that can keep you in fear. The worst thing that might happen is that you learn something new about yourself. There is no failure, just a diversion on the path to learning. Everything you do adds to your knowledge and experience.

9. **Challenge**: Of course, there will be challenges in your life. That's one of the reasons you are here—to learn all that you can about

who you are. The key question to ask yourself whenever you are in a personal crisis is: "What can I learn from this experience? Am I still buried in the fear of an illness, a loss, or deep sadness? Or is there something that I can discover about myself from this situation?" Challenges can also be ones that we initiate in order to learn a new skill, a new life direction, or a new way of overcoming a fear. If we originate this growth, it brings strong elements of joy and self-confidence into our physical, emotional, and spiritual bodies. This is the greatest learning tool of all—self-empowered evolution. We do not need a life-threatening challenge to grow. Our inner soul-self, who grows and learns along with us in the physical world, becomes ecstatic with self-chosen transformation because it is always more fun and so much gentler. Thrive on challenges. You are in Earth School, so there will always be challenges. Which ones have been the most fun for you? Which ones did you invite into your life? Which ones came without invitation?

10. **Celebration**: Love life! Love life! Love life! Life is a gift. Live it to its fullest. Take no prisoners! Maximize your time here and become all that you desire to be. And, when you have reached that sacred place of manifestation, share it with others so that their internal *fire* may be lit by your renewed personal passion. You will become that which you feel you deeply deserve. Celebrate! Each day is a gift!

Don't pursue happiness. Create it.
Chinese proverb

"Choose your thoughts wisely, because they are the energy that create your life."

~ Abraham Hicks

www.PeaceInThePresentMoment.net

Michele Penn
copyright 2012

(Courtesy of Michele Penn and Abraham Hicks)

CHAPTER 10

TOOL 3

The Law of Attraction

For forty-three years, as a spiritual seeker, I sought out books, workshops, DVDs, and CDs on Jesus' life, the Ascended Masters, guardian angels, and the Dalai Lama to learn how to more closely connect to the spiritual aspect of myself. I was delving into the various teachings to discover what resonated with me. I studied with gifted intuitives, spiritual teachers, and highly advanced channels from Los Angeles to New York City.

Then, about 15 years ago, I found Esther and Jerry Hicks, and Abraham. Their story is absolutely fascinating. Esther and Jerry were a couple from San Antonio, Texas, who started to meditate together because Jerry (who sadly passed away in 2011) was enamored with the concept of universal consciousness and all of the knowledge that he could access from that source. For about nine months they meditated daily. Esther meditated not because it was her passion but because it was so important to Jerry, and he wanted them to do it together. She was somewhat interested but not as passionate as her husband. But, surprise, surprise—Esther was the one who started receiving messages from angelic presences when she was in a quiet, meditative state. Jerry wrote down the communiques. He was so excited and thrilled that they had made a connection. He started to ask questions of the entities who called themselves Abraham as a group, and Esther became more and more proficient at translating the knowledge she was receiving.

Esther was receiving this profound, universal wisdom more clearly every day, and she began to help family and friends. Jerry started to audiotape the sessions so that they would have a complete record of what was said. Their story began to unfold with larger and larger audiences, and now Esther is sought after worldwide to present the teachings of Abraham, the group of angelic masters who so love humanity that they want us to know that they are with us every minute of every day.

Their teachings are based on the Law of Attraction, which states that what you think, you will receive. Amazing! So simple but not so easy to understand and put into practice because we, as humans, have to change the way we think. Our goal each day needs to be about finding that *good feeling thought*. For yourself, if you are constantly grateful for all you have, you will have more of that for which you are grateful. And, vice versa, that which you don't want will continue to come to you if your predominant thought pattern is on the negative.

Abraham and Esther Hicks Words of Wisdom (A limited interpretation)

I could never do Esther and Abraham's work justice in the short synopsis in this book. It is so comprehensive and personally directed to each of us that my experience would probably not be your experience. There is so much fabulous information that I would like to direct you to the website: www.abraham-hicks.com. What I will do here is give you *my* interpretation of what I have learned and how I am trying to apply this transforming knowledge to my life.

- The Law of Attraction: Your thoughts are magnetic. What you think, positive or negative, will draw the same type of experiences back to you.

- You are the physical manifestation of the all-loving non-physical world, and your work here is to seek joy and use your freedom of choice to discover all things in life that bring you that joy. You are spirit *first*, having a physical experience. You are here to create a life of great joy and celebrate that creation with all of those you love and meet along the way.

- Your emotions are the guideposts that let you know if your thoughts are "feeling good" or positive, or "not feeling good" or negative. When you *choose* to *change* (see the Ten Sacred Insights in chapter 9) your thoughts, then your emotions will change. If you concentrate on your positive, changed thought for 17 seconds, it will become part of your daily thought pattern. (I use my sport watch or cell phone to time myself.) When I veer back into unwanted emotions (not feeling good), I go into my mind and look for that visual, good-feeling thought and give it 17 seconds of concentration for at total of 68 seconds at a time.

- You are the ultimate creator of your life. Each and every situation you are in has been created by you. "How can that be?" I asked myself that question when I had cancer. My thoughts continually created negative energy that surrounded my cell membranes when I told myself how much I hated my job and how I couldn't get out of what I was doing because of prior financial obligations, fear, etc. I created that negative environment, and it took its toll on my health (see my first book, *Bootstraps*, page 18). For five years, all I did was complain to myself and my husband about how much I really hated my job. It took cancer for me to quit.

- You can *create anything* that you are passionate about. The more passionate you are about what you desire, the faster that desired dream will come to you. As you go along, you may want to divest yourself of negative aspects in your life—job, relationships, living location—to find the path to passionate positivity. As an example, I want to expand the amenities at our ranch to train more horses in our effort to help our returning veterans and their families find a new future for themselves. We need a covered riding arena to keep out the rain, the intense heat, and the snow and ice. I am continually shaping my thoughts to help me visualize large sums of money. (I do not care where it comes from, I am not picky.) $200,000 (or more of course) sounds just about right! My dreams are a work in progress.

- We never get it all done, meaning that life will continually give us new challenges for change. Change is good. It's what keeps us passionate about life and keeps us exploring new heights of growth. Remember that the more positive expectation you have of your future experiences, the more positive they will be.

- Gratitude! What are you grateful for right this minute? The more grateful you are, the more you will receive that for which you are grateful. Money? Good health? Loving relationships? If you don't have what you dearly desire, go a few steps beyond where you are right now in your thoughts and imagine what it *feels* like to be in that new, wonderful receiving place. For 17 seconds. Again and again.

CHAPTER 11

Get out of your comfort zone

"You must do the thing you think you cannot do."
Eleanor Roosevelt

What is a comfort zone, and why would I want to get out of it? I worked *really* hard to create this comfort zone, a comfy place of protection from the past, and *I do not* want to leave it. But, the caveat is that I get bored when life is not challenging me in some way to participate on a larger scale.

There are times, of course, when we want to stay in our comfort zones because of traumatic situations that have a grip on us. For the most part, instances of unwanted drama should be few and far between. What we want to be searching for are ways to ignite our passion so that the passionate challenge lifts us out of our comfort zone naturally.

When days start to feel humdrum, I have to ask myself what pattern have I gotten into that is unfulfilling. Perhaps, it's not taking a chance to do something differently when I have the chance. Or, perhaps, it's always playing it safe—following the rules that someone else has set down for me. I don't like rules. I grew up a military brat and all I ever lived by were rules. I didn't feel free. I wanted to grow and expand and learn new languages, meet new people, try new food, take on new challenges. So, what did I do? I *married* into the military. Wow! I solved that problem, didn't I?

Expect the Extraordinary

What this new marriage challenge did was incite me to learn to think for myself. My husband was away in Vietnam and, later, on many other military training exercises, so that I had to "grow up" and not depend on anyone else to think for me. I LOVED that new freedom. *I was learning to leave the protection of the past behind.*

But, as time went by, I again felt like I was in a prison of my own making. How do I keep going back to this place of total dissatisfaction? After realizing that what I was looking for was passion in life, I searched for any direction that could propel me on a path of taking more risks. No matter how large or small, a personal risk infuses us with excitement when it is calculated and well researched. I don't mean taking a mindless risk just for the sake of pushing yourself into a dangerous predicament. The steps I take are, first, I ask my heart (where intuition lives) if I intuitively find taking this risk expanding for me. Then, I ask my solar plexus (place of personal power) if this opportunity is going to help me grow, or is it going to shut me down because it is too much. Learning to ride a horse at age sixty was a very calculated risk. It was challenging, exciting, and launched me into realizing that each calculated risk was a chance for personal growth. "Faith and fear cannot occupy the same space." (See Melisa Pearce's book, *Touched by a Horse*.)

One of the other surprising motivating factors that "showed up" for me to bring about change was the movie, *Bucket List*. A bucket list is an inventory of adventures that you deeply desire to experience and that light up your life! That film ignited a feeling in me telling me that I was missing out on something in my life. Would my life get to its close without my having realized all the excitement I wanted to invite into my reality? So, I started to write down bits and pieces of ideas that would really expand my passion for living, to be completed by age ninety. It looked something like this:

- **Take a trip to Paris, the city of love, with the beloved of my life, my husband, John.** True romance didn't enter my life until

I was sixty-four, and I want to experience everything wonderful in this world with this extraordinary man. (More about this relationship later in the book.)

- **Gallop across a field on my horse without fear.** I am afraid of speed on anything, but particularly on a horse, which I can't always control. Overcoming this fear of speed is a primary goal in my life.

- **Speak to groups across the country on how to find their Path of Passion**[sm]**.** I love speaking to groups to help them discover greater passion in their lives by taking chances to live more fearlessly.

- **Publish more books (this book is number two out of four).** Writing is my way of communicating with the world to make a difference. I find passionate creativity by putting my thoughts and emotions down on paper.

- **Build a larger Livin' the Dream Ranch to accommodate more veterans and their families for healing by using the wisdom of the horses.** Making a difference in someone else's life is the greatest *high* one can experience. Our veterans and their families have sacrificed more than most of us can ever imagine. They deserve loving support from their country. Livin' the Dream Ranch, our Virginia facility, offers veterans and their families a way to become more empowered by partnering with an equine mentor.

This is just the beginning of my bucket list. I hope it changes each day as I strive to absorb all of the wonderful opportunities this list offers me. What is your bucket list? How far along are you with yours? Start today! Writing it down commits you to a stronger commitment of action. Writing it down is a more solid energy than just visualizing it.

When I was researching how to build my bucket list for my blog, so I could post on our website, www.livinthedreamranch.com, I came across a review of a best seller entitled, *The Top Five Regrets of the Dying*, by Bronnie Ware, a palliative care nurse. She helps patients in the last phase of their lives. Her book is terrific, and seeing that I have a 93-year-old mother, her work has helped me immeasurably. Listed below are the "Five Regrets" she has seen in her many years of working with the dying. What follows here is a brief summary of her thoughts and mine.

1. I wish I'd had the courage to live a life true to myself, not the life others expected of me. This was the most common regret reported in the research. While most of us have our health now, it is time to take chances in life and live what *we* most want. Most of the folks who answered these questions had not lived even half of their dreams.

My mother is ninety-three, and when I go to the retirement home where she lives, I see so many elderly people living in such sadness of incomplete lives. There are so many experiences that my mother says she has missed, and now she lives in regret. This is such a teaching moment for me. Every time I leave from seeing her, I tell myself to live my life more fully. Stop procrastinating!

2. I wish I hadn't worked so hard. This came from every male patient that the author had taken care of. And many women answered "yes" as well. Did we work too hard and not play enough? I think of all the moments I missed with my children when they were growing up. As a wife with a husband at war, I was so caught up in getting all of my household chores done that I didn't stop to play. I don't make that mistake with my grandchildren. *I play a lot, and it feels so good.*

3. I wish I had stayed in touch with my friends. Many of the seniors had lost friendships as they aged, and they deeply regretted it. My growing up years as an army brat had me moving every three years to a new location. This led me to make friends knowing I wouldn't have them in my life for long. As an adult, I have missed out on maintaining friendships because I have also moved often. In the last several years, I have changed that pattern and have wonderful relationships that thrive through emails and phone calls even when we live in different cities.

4. I wish I had the courage to express my feelings. Many people don't speak up in order to not offend others. What it keeps them from doing is being true to themselves. Keeping feelings inside can lead to anger and resentment, and even be the cause of illness. When we are younger, we probably often felt others defined us. But as we grow older, we find our voices and realize that we were not born attached at the hip to our parents, our spouses, or our bosses. We live for ourselves. We learn to speak with an authentic voice.

5. I wish that I had let myself be happier. Happiness is a choice, and most people don't realize that staying in old patterns can keep them from living life fully. Taking *chances* for making new *choices* can bring wonderful, new life *challenges*! Change your old habits and you change your life! When you realize you are fully responsible for your own happiness, you begin to take steps to make that happiness blossom every day.

From the newspaper of May 4, 2015: *"Pursue your passions, and live longer—Got a great reason to jump out of bed in the morning? Only 37 percent of North Americans say they do, according to a recent Gallup Poll. But a new study might motivate you to find your sense of purpose: Turns out having a mission in life can help you become healthier and live longer."* These are the words of Dr. Mehmet Oz, famed heart transplant surgeon, and Dr. Michael Roizen, chief wellness officer at the Cleveland Clinic. I've followed Dr. Oz long before he became famous with Oprah's help.

There is no passion to be found in settling for a life that is less than the one you are capable of living.
Nelson Mandela

Going against all odds at Columbia Presbyterian Hospital in New York, Dr. Oz allowed a hands-on energy healer in his transplant operating room before he began surgery to help the patient accept the new heart. This highly talented surgeon invited a very gifted hands-on energy healer, Julie Motz, into his pre-op surgery suite to help the incoming heart and the outgoing one to adjust to their new surroundings. She whispered to the new heart (see The HeartMath Institute's research about the heart's brain) that it was loved and would be helped by the doctor and his team into their new lives. The damaged heart would pass on quietly and peacefully leaving struggle behind, and the new transplanted heart would be treasured and welcomed in its new body. Dr.Oz's patients' recuperative rate far exceeded his expectations. His wife, Lisa, is a Reiki healer; Reiki is an ancient hands-on healing modality from Japan.

To sum up, what I am so anxious to impart to you is to *live your life with joy and exhilaration NOW. It belongs only to you!*

part four

WHERE AM I TODAY?

Bella and Skye

CHAPTER 12

From heartbeats to hoofbeats: discovering my age of authenticity

Don't follow where the path may lead. . . .
Go where there is no path and leave a trail.
Ralph Waldo Emerson

For over forty years I have searched for ways to find an ongoing bond with those angelic beings that saved my life. As I mentioned in Part III, I took workshops, became certified as an intuitive healer and clinical hypnotherapist, and worked with my hands as an energy healer for those who needed healing in specific areas of their bodies. I was looking for any and all ways to be in that sacred space of connection.

When I turned sixty, I was still searching for a new direction that would put me on a path to greater spiritual fulfillment and, at the same time, would be an exciting challenge. But, most importantly, the new direction had to be a step on a path to passionate living; that path of passion is what the angels called living in your "age of authenticity." I could feel, in my heart space, the deep urging to live as if every day were a gift because human life could disappear in an instant. The three life-saving angelic encounters were now profoundly part of my being. I knew my next goal was to find ways to expand myself—in my learning, my loving, my living.

On a warm afternoon in July 2004 in Tisbury, Massachusetts, I went with a friend to visit a barn where my friend's niece was taking horseback riding lessons. It was a beautiful location spread out over several acres with a gorgeous, silver light lake just beyond the riding arenas. We went into the barn to look around.

I had been near a horse only once in my life and had no idea what I was doing when I was asked if I wanted to ride. Without any riding instructions or guidance, I got on a horse. The horse didn't like the trail buddy in front of him, and it proceeded to rear up and dump me on the ground. I just got up laughing because the horse was so gentle about it; I just slowly slid off his back.

The barn in Tisbury was very different from most horse barns. These horses were being trained for competition and a riding school. The first horse I met was a huge bay, probably seventeen hands (really big) named Amar. What a sweetheart! I could feel his energy around humans. He really liked the human species. He put his head over the stall door and breathed on my face, sniffing me. I was completely smitten. I wanted to be connected to this 1,200 pound playmate.

I asked one of the trainers if she gave lessons. She said that in July and August they were totally booked with kids' lessons, but in September I could join an adult's class. I didn't want to wait. I wasn't sure I would be there in September. I asked if I could learn to ride with the kids' beginners' class. The trainer very hesitantly said yes. I know she thought I was crazy, but, there was something in that horse's eyes. It was mesmerizing. I was feeling "complete" somehow.

I was discovering an entirely new life path at the ripe old age of sixty that would propel me into a future of deep love, occasional fear, and fathomless connection to something spiritually greater than I was. I found my angelic connection in the soul of a horse. Our angels come to us in the form we can most easily connect with.

From first meeting Amar, to learning to ride with the six-year olds, to returning to my home in Florida and finding a natural horsemanship trainer, to meeting Skye, my first horse when I was sixty-two, the journey has been, and still is, extraordinary. I have been exhilarated by learning something new that the horse and I could discover together, and I have been scared to death at being dangerously dumped, resulting in a badly pulled groin ligament and severe concussion. But, what a wealth of knowledge has been given to me. I have learned so much about the inside of a horse—his heart, his soul, his passion for being here on earth to help and guide human beings.

A horse is a truly magnificent being representing the finest of Mother Nature and her love of humankind. The horse is the second most spiritual animal, after an elephant. In the earlier chapter, "Donnie's Conversation with God," Donnie was given information about elephants and hors*es—both are here to carry us and teach us to carry ourselves* by overcoming our fears.

What I mean by *carry* is that when you are on the back of a 1,200 pound animal and you and the animal are in sync together, you feel you can do anything. These large animals teach us to *carry* ourselves steeped in self-esteem and self-confidence, which are the calling cards of a fully blossoming human. As we face our fear of mounting such a huge animal, we face all of our fears—fear of failure, fear of an accident, fear of never "getting it," and, ultimately, fear of death or the unknown.

This is why horses are considered spiritual; they are the ultimate teachers and mirrors for you and for me. The horse, as a mentor, forces us to face ourselves and our own shortcomings, because it has no ego and, therefore, no shortcomings. A horse lives simply in black and white. What you see is what you get. You better know what you are getting into when you join up in partnership with a horse. The horse expects you to live by your word and respect yourself and, most importantly, respect the horse.

Why would you, the reader, be interested in how a horse thinks or acts? What I have discovered over the past ten years is that an interaction with a horse is representative of, and fully reflects back to us, how we enter and engage in human relationships. Are you pushy and low on patience? Do you baby your relationships instead of speaking up with an authentic voice of truth? If you baby a horse, you have a bully waiting to emerge. You must learn to lead in your equine relationship with authority, just as you would in your personal life, even if only leading yourself and no one else. Do you reflect love and kindness in word and deed? Horses crave sweet whispers of love. Their ears and eyes perk up, just like a baby's, when you speak in soft whispers. Horses never reflect that they are victims. They don't complain about what life offers them; they just learn to live with it and make their lives better by starting over with fresh eyes and ears at the dawn of the new day. They don't hold grudges. They are committed to their herd, both equine and human, when members of the herd have earned that commitment from them.

Isn't it the same for you, in your human commitments? Don't you want to be able to speak openly and honestly, to be able to love unconditionally and to be understood regardless of the circumstances?

The horse and the human are remarkably alike. Love is the deepest and most powerful energy on the planet. The horse reflects that for us all in its love of physical freedom and the protection of its herd. If you saw The Belmont race on June 6, 2015, the last of the Triple Crown races this year, you watched American Pharaoh run, a horse that loves to run for himself and his humans. Regardless of your thoughts about horse racing, that animal was the finest example of a path of passion I have ever seen. He ran for the total love of the freedom of what his body loved to do. What do you love to do in your life that reflects your unbridled path of passion?

As the past ten years have progressed, Skye, my first horse, has been with me during a spouse's death, a remarriage, a move from Florida to Virginia, and so many other life changes. And, I have been with her during her wild, early mare years, and then during the birth of her baby, Bella, in 2014. What a great mommy she has become and what a great example of unconditional love in nature. Skye has taught me so much about how to live my life authentically, with purpose and poise. I want to share with you what both she and Bella have taught me.

Skye's Secrets for Success

- Why are you rushing through life? Are you anxious to leave? Take your time, life will be here tomorrow. Don't rush saddling me and rush getting off of me. Enjoy our time together. *Let's spend some time together really getting to know each other.* When you look into my eyes, you will see my soul which is always filled with love for you.

- *Trust yourself to know what is best for you and for me.* I know you are not perfect, but I also know you are trying to do the best you can. That is good enough for me.

- I will teach you when you are doing something wrong—I will shake my head, pull on the bit in my mouth, or try to ride out from under you. So, it would be wise to "think before you act. *Trust your intuition in all of life* but particularly when you are on my back.

- *Challenge yourself every day*, and we will have more fun together.

- *Before you can adequately lead me, you must be able to lead yourself.* Get to know yourself well. I am a mirror to you for your successes and misdirections. I will show you where you may want to enhance your life's path.

- *For you to be successful in life, you must be responsible for your thoughts and actions.* Do not blame me for your mistakes or your lack of knowledge. I respond to the rider's lead.

- I am the perfect example of the Law of Attraction: what you put out in your thoughts is what response you will get back from me in the form of actions. *Fear begets fear. Love begets love. Confidence begets confidence.*

- I can teach you on the ground or in the saddle. I was born to teach my human partner how to live a full life of self-love. *When you are confident within yourself, I sense that energy and I, therefore, become confident in myself.*

A concept from the ancient Hermetic writings of *The Emerald Tablet,* a time capsule of wisdom, says, "As above, so below." The concept that we can create heaven on earth by our thoughts and actions is exactly what happens in the saddle. As I give clear positive directions from above, sitting in the saddle, the horse below me offers me heaven on earth as a partnership of life's dance.

Beautiful Bella's Blessing
When Skye was about eight, she acted as though she was pining for other mares' foals when she saw them running in the fields in Florida. I wondered if she wanted a baby of her own. I let that thought go because there were so many pressing matters in my life at the time. My husband had passed away earlier. Two years later, I met John Pighini and moved to Virginia where we married and built a beautiful horse farm. I just watched as Skye blossomed with daily attention from us both. She was so much happier here in Virginia than being boarded forty-five minutes away from me outside of Sarasota, Florida.

One day my daughter and granddaughters made the two-hour trip to visit us. Sammie, who was almost four at the time, loved

Skye and would always try to give her kisses on her nose. Skye just thought Sammie was the cat's meow. She would sniff her, nuzzle her neck and reach over the fence to try to get closer to that human baby. Again, I wondered if the mare wanted to be pregnant and have a baby of her own.

Fast forward to May 2013. John and I decided that this mare, Skye, really wanted to be a mother. So, we found a local facility that could artificially inseminate her. We wanted the father (sire) to be Duals Warpaint, a particularly athletic stallion from Ocala, Florida, who had a wonderful disposition, loved to run, and had a competitive drive. For this reason, we had his refrigerated sperm shipped overnight for artificial insemination in Skye. She was impregnated May 24, 2013.

She had an easy pregnancy but a very long one—twelve months. Horses normally deliver within 11 months of being impregnated, but Skye's was definitely taking longer. As we got closer to the delivery date, we watched her closely. John and I took turns living in our horse trailer outside the barn where we had a video receiver for cameras set up in the barn. We *had* to see this momentous event. All the books said that the first foal is usually delivered between two and five a.m. To say we were really sleep deprived would be understating the condition we were in.

Then, one night, we decided to eat dinner together for the first time in a week, late for us, at about 8:30. John finished eating and said, "I better go check on Skye. I feel something funny about her." I said ok, and that I'd do the dishes and be right over. He left and two minutes later yelled, "Get over here, we have a baby on the ground." I ran over to the barn with a dishtowel still in my hand to watch the last of the delivery, as Skye was cleaning up our beautiful Bella. Skye was such an attentive mother, checking Bella all over, licking her, nuzzling her, and watching her every move.

We just stood back and took it all in with absolute awe. Bella stood on her wobbly legs and about an hour later found her way to nursing on her mommy. We then knew that all was well. Her legs were sturdy, and she and her mom were bonding beautifully. The vet arrived soon to pronounce daughter and mother gorgeous and doing splendidly. Whew! What a chance we took, knowing absolutely nothing about breeding our mare and delivering a foal. We did it with the help of lots of veterinarians' web postings and lots of books. We have not regretted it for one single moment. Bella has taught us so much about love and softness in life.

We realized, after Bella was born, that we were in the midst of learning true inter-species communication. Bella taught us to communicate through softness—soft touch, soft voice, soft and slow introduction to something very new, the human world. There were no aggressive or fast moves. That scares a horse and particularly a very young one. Maybe this is a way for each of us to treat each other—soft feel without aggression.

Bella has been an absolute blessing. She has guided us into being in the present moment—paying attention to each second that we are in these human bubbles called bodies. If you are not aware around horses, they can step on you, bump you, and do whatever it takes to get your attention. Bella's unconditional trust in us, a very different species, is so humbling. How could we ever misuse that trust? How could we ever dishonor the fact that she has entrusted us with her life? Very humbling, indeed. When we form relationships, either human or animal, we each are committing ourselves to the welfare of the other. If we learn to communicate with a voice of loving authenticity, we will always have the trust of the other.

This is how the angels speak, with voices of loving truthfulness to keep us guided and safe. Perhaps, Bella is an equine angel sent to teach us love and joy. Thank you, beautiful Bella!

Dr. Deborah McCormick
(Courtesy of Dr. Deborah McCormick)

CHAPTER 13

The experts speak

While I was researching why angelic *animal* messengers come into our lives for this section of the book, I knew I wanted the expertise of those who have spoken and worked with animals all of their lives. What is the "spiritual" aspect of a horse or an elephant or a dog? What does that mean in terms of an animal's place on the earth? Why are they here? I will introduce you to three extraordinary teachers and mentors who completely live their lives in the animal and human spiritual world that I lovingly inhabit.

Dr. Marlena Deborah McCormick,
Tres Aquilas Hacienda (Three Eagles)

Dr. Marlena Deborah McCormick, a gifted psychologist, along with her mother, Dr. Adele von Rust McCormick, also a gifted horse woman and psychologist, and her father, Dr. Tom McCormick, a psychiatrist, wrote one of the most fascinating and inspiring books on the relationship between humans and horses I have ever read, *Horse Sense and the Human Heart*, (published in 2010 by HCI, www.horsesenseandthehumanheart.com). I read this book before I had taken my first riding lesson or acquired my first horse. This book showed me the path to finding an angelic connection on earth through the heart of a horse.

The concept that a horse of 1,000 pounds or more has the intuition to guide me in life was amazing. If you study the anatomy of a horse, its heart can be as large as 22 pounds, like the famous racehorse Secretariat, or all of eight to ten pounds, as in a normal horse. A human's heart is ten to twelve ounces. If we can believe that our intuition lives not only in our thoughts (nervous system) but originates in our heart, then we can surmise that a horse's intuition is ten times that of a human being. Horses need that intuition to keep them safe in the wild; always being able to sense danger has been hard-wired into their DNA. When they interact with us, they can tell intuitively by our emotions and the energy from those emotions—happy, sad, angry, or high-strung from using alcohol or drugs—how safe they are in our world. In the work that I do with clients at our ranch in Virginia, Livin' the Dream Ranch, the horse chooses the person with whom to partner in order to help that human heal. Amazing work! The horses know which in their herd of four has the greatest gift to offer an individual sitting in the arena. It is their divine path to connect with us to help us see the "bigger picture" for our lives. Where are we going and why? Does this path give us joy or grief? ARE WE HAPPY WITH OUR CHOICES?

Horse Sense and the Human Heart offers us the absolute best view of how horses really *feel* about us as *their person*. They can have many human partners in their equine/human family, but only one person will be *their person*. It's a wonderful book with inspiring insights. I hope you get a chance to read the McCormick's seminal work on how horses help humans heal. The Drs. McCormick are long-time breeders, trainers, and lovers of Peruvian horses, which are ideal for therapy work because of their gentle, gregarious and spirited nature.

When I asked Dr. Deborah McCormick (with whom I studied for eighteen months on the psychology of how we can partner with horses for human healing) to answer some questions from my client base, she responded with some of the most fascinating answers, based on her years of experience helping humans find their path to healing using equine wisdom. Below are the questions and my paraphrasing of her answers.

1. How intuitive/spiritual are horses versus other animals?

All animals touch different aspects of who we are. They light up our passion for living and connect us to the source of our real being. We can acquire greater compassion for others and animals alike. In this understanding, all animals are spiritual.

2. What is a horse's "big picture," spiritual purpose for being on earth?

The horse has a refined ability to see who we actually are—what our talents are as well as our shortcomings. Through the eye of the equine, we can address our personal issues and also celebrate our heart-driven gifts. The horse invites us to welcome and nurture all parts of ourselves, both the fearful moments and those that celebrate our learning about who we are and what we can achieve. They entice us to nourish our authentic selves by living outside our comfort zones and reaching for adventures along side of them that could birth our fearlessness in life. The quest in a human/equine relationship is to gain greater wisdom about oneself.

3. What does a horse want from a relationship with a human?

The equine world deeply desires a relationship with humans who are "real" or authentic in their feelings. These authentic people live from the inside out, not the other way around. A horse gravitates to people who are genuine and who have a great heart and higher mind. The horse connects to people who think deeply and who look inside themselves for the answers they seek. The equine has a high level of sensitivity, and therefore mistrusts humans who are arrogant, live falsehoods, lack discipline, and have hidden agendas—those people use the horse as a vehicle to promote their egos. In order to gain a horse's trust, we must live authentically—fear is fear, happiness is happiness, love is love. Authenticity shows all honesty.

4. What can we learn from the horse regarding living the fullest life possible?
A horse that retains its personality and spirit can teach humans to live expansively but sensibly. Do not take chances that you are not ready for—a horse doesn't. It won't go over a stream unless it feels secure that it is safe, and that his rider is the best leader for him. But, often, humans try to shut down the spirit of the horse out of their own fear. The horse teaches us to address our anxiety by taking calculated risks as we learn to go forward in life. The horse develops its spiritual nature of joy, love, and fun without sacrificing its instincts, passion, and intuition. This is great learning for us: Learn to live life expansively and passionately by taking *calculated, learned* risks. Be brave but be safe!

5. What would you want the reader to learn about the horse/human connection?
Dr. McCormick says, "To befriend a horse is a unique and magnificent journey into a world of surprises, epiphanies and unfolding kinships. On this adventure, we find meaning, mystery and beauty. We find hope and challenges. We learn to value chaos and rest. We discover the power of simplicity and concentration. We realize it is all good. We begin to understand the deeper significance of the words in the Book of John—'I call you friends.'"

6. What would you want the reader to know about your work?
"Our aim is to offer human beings an opportunity to wake up and feel more alive. We hope people will regain their sense of wonder and awe. When this happens, human beings discover an empowering vision and a greater desire to soar. By learning to appreciate, understand and contemplate the complex and dynamic nature of

the human heart and mind, we can rejoin the cosmic community and march in the grand procession" [of life in the Universe].

Please visit Drs. McCormick's website at www.horsesenseandthehumanheart.com for their newest on-site and online courses. Their wisdom on how to live a victorious life is inspiring.

R'Delle Anderson
(Courtesy of R'Delle Anderson)

The experts speak

R'Delle Anderson, Essentially Soul

For more than forty years I have searched for gifted intuitives to help guide me along my path of exploration for greater angelic connection. I have worked with more than a dozen clairvoyant channels all over the country. During each of these learning relationships, I have birthed new careers, moved to new locations, changed unhealthy relationships, and diligently studied how to grow into my own skin and become my own personal guide.

One of the most influential teachers and mentors I have had is R'Delle Anderson. R'Delle knew as a young child she was different; she could see colored auras around people as they sat in church. She loved animals, and she became *a straw through which animals and people could draw energy.* She is highly gifted, able to "see" into the souls of her clients with the help and guidance of the Ascended Masters (spiritually enlightened beings who have had at least one lifetime/incarnation on earth) and archangels (angels at the highest level of learning who assist humanity to fulfill their paths of enlightened spiritual growth). R'Delle brings out the highest good of each client, helping them see themselves in a new light of excitement of what is possible for them. She is in constant connection with your specific angel guides when she talks to you, the interpreter for you to find the light inside of you to live an extraordinary life.

R'Delle has studied so many spiritual modalities: Reiki, Shamanism, acupressure, energy work, and light work. She is licensed as a social worker, psychologist, and private therapist. Her only desire is for you to believe that there is more to you and your path than you ever realized. She has helped to affirm in me that I am on the right path with my writing, my equine healing program, and my mentoring women who are on their paths to greater self-realization.

I asked R'Delle several questions, and I think you will find her answers fascinating, as well as helpful in understanding that you are never alone and are always in connection with *your* angelic partners or other "light being" partners, either in animal form or ethereal form. Here are the questions and R'Delle's direct answers, as well as a few comments from me.

1. What can one do to connect with one's angelic presences?

"Have you ever felt you were just 'in the flow' or 'in the zone'? That place is known as your 'I Am Presence'—your connection to All That Is, to the Divine Presence, to the Ascended Masters/Archangels/Other Light Beings. It can happen most easily when you bring your attention to your breath. Take a long deep breath, in through your nose, as you envision or feel yourself drawing the breath down through the crown chakra at the top of your head. Then, draw the breath down through the body, pausing at the 'still point'—that place where you are no longer inhaling but have not yet started exhaling—and hold your breath for just a moment before you exhale through your heart space. The 'still point' is your place of connection to All That Is. The more you quietly breathe in this 'still point' manner, the more you can connect on a daily or momentary basis. Your 'I Am Presence' is connecting you to your Higher Self and to the universal 'I Am' of God and all angelic messengers and other guides."

2. How do we know if an angelic presence is near us?

"Your angelic presences want so deeply to connect with you. They may drop a book on your toe, or have a magazine catch your eye, or excite you about a movie. These are the many ways that they can attract your attention in a human way. In a more ethereal way, they may get your attention with a fleeting light gliding by your peripheral vision, or perhaps you hear someone whispering to you and there is no one near you, or perhaps a certain scent gets your attention. These are just signs that they are present and available to assist you."

Author comment: I, personally, smell the same scent when I am near certain other women. I could be in a food store, a bookstore, or a movie theater when a woman passes me and I smell that same scent. I am still working on what it means, but am pretty sure it has something to do with their health. I also know when the angels want me to pay close attention because butterflies will come out in full force. I have come to know that this butterfly message is about something happening in the near future. I am to have wide eyes for seeing what is about to transpire around me.

3. How did you first recognize the presence of angels, guides, or Ascended Masters?

"I think I have known that I was not alone, that I was protected, since I was very young, maybe four years old or so. I don't have any specific memories, just a knowingness. When I was a bit older, maybe seven or eight, I remember holding a little bird that was hurt and feeling my hands become very hot and seeing the bird recover. I knew it wasn't me—it wasn't me making my hands hot, it wasn't me healing the bird. It was through me, not of me, and I knew it was good!"

4. How could someone else learn to connect?

"By believing! By opening ourselves to the unlimited possibilities of all that is, by accepting that there are miracles around us all the time. If God/All That Is is truly omniscient, omnipotent, and omnipresent, then it is about believing that the only thing in the way of connecting to these wonderful angelic presences or Light Beings is us—we, ourselves. If we get out of our own way, allowing ourselves to go into our I Am Presence (our God-like presence) through deep breathing, meditating, prayer, or quiet reflection in nature, we open ourselves to this gift of amazing Love and Light."

5. By being connected, do we learn more about fearless living?

"Yes! When we realize and trust that we are not alone but are being guided by these amazing angelic presences, we can tap into our own higher selves and learn to recognize the call from our spiritual guides. We are not puppets in some grand play, but active co-creators of our lives. When we pay attention to a message, then we can go into our own High Heart, located at the thymus gland in the center of the chest, and discern whether or not it is our call to act upon that message.

The Masters are clear that there are no "wrong" decisions—only decisions that offer us a whole other set of opportunities/possibilities. We always have free will, but when we then decide to move forward on the messages/information we receive from our High Heart, our Higher Self, then we are acting on the guidance we have received from our connection to the Divine. This method of tuning in, paying attention to our connection to the Divine, is very empowering. It has a rhythm to it—trust that you are not alone. Wait for the messages of guidance, hear them through your High Heart to discern if this is right for you. Then, with empowered thought, know that you have made the best possible choice for yourself."

Author comment: I want to mention something that may help you with connecting to this guidance. I have been working with angelic presences for more than forty years, most of the time not even knowing what I was doing. Now, I do know, by how my body feels. When I am connecting and it is a good decision for me, I will feel a heightened sense of energy and excitement. I feel good. If it is a decision that is not in my best interest, I will feel shut down and anxious. For me to feel anything in the way of guidance, I must have quiet. No TV, no music, no outside conversation. Just me and my guidance system, the Law of Attraction at work.

6. What message would you want to convey to your audience in *Expect the Extraordinary*?

"We each, I believe, are truly unique and have our own path to follow. It is hard, sometimes, to even see our own gifts, let alone honor them. From my perspective, we all specifically agreed to be here on this planet now, at this time. I work with the Archangels (extraordinary beings, extensions of God himself, see https://en.wikipedia.org/wiki/Archangel), Ascended Masters and other Light Beings. The Ascended Masters are essentially spiritually enlightened Beings who have had at least one lifetime/incarnation here on Earth. These Masters have moved forward on their own ascension (spiritual growth) journey (reincarnating many lifetimes), moving through a series of spiritual transformations in their own right. They are committed to assisting in our ascension process. These Masters tell us that our souls reside (live) at the frequency of joy *all the time* on the inner planes (a state of consciousness that transcends the known physical universe). Our work, our agreement, our soul contract—however you want to view it—is about bringing that frequency of joy into our lives as often as possible and sustaining it for as long as possible. Our work is to follow in the footsteps of Christ and Buddha and Allah and BE the Light of the world."

R'Delle Anderson can be reached for phone sessions at (707) 845-2715; essentiallysoul@gmail.com; www.essentiallysoul.com.

Expect the Extraordinary

Diane Roadcap

The experts speak

Diane Roadcap, Animal Communicator
"Animals Awaken Our Hearts"

As a child, Diane knew she had a special relationship with animals, large and small. She would play with a variety of creatures around her home near Washington, D.C. She discovered she could connect with them at a soul level, reading their deepest needs and wants. Her "gift" really became more heightened when, at age five, her dog, Blackie, warned her telepathically that a poisonous snake was perilously close to her and she should back up slowly and get out of the impending danger.

As an adult, Diane worked in the corporate world, but always felt a yearning to be back in those Virginia woods communicating with the dogs, cats, squirrels, and nature's other friends. So, what did she do? She followed her passion and left corporate America. She has become one of the premier animal communicators in the country. She is called upon not only by pet owners, but also by the police looking for lost or stolen animals. Diane is also a frequent guest lecturer at the exquisite spa, Canyon Ranch, in Lenox, Massachusetts, where guests bring their pets for readings with Diane. She also holds workshops on animal communication at Canyon Ranch.

Diane truly enhanced the life of one of my horses, Nic, when she explained why he was so anxious and scared in 2014 after he ran so fast that I had to jump off when I couldn't control him. He was injured, but we couldn't see the injury. He was trying to run away from the pain. She later explained to me that Nic was trained for a certain sport, barrel racing, way too early at the very young age of four. He was disciplined very aggressively when he didn't learn as fast as the owner wanted. This explained why Nic was so scared all the time and very "spooky" at anything. He didn't trust humans to take care of him. There was such sadness in his eyes. If it hadn't been for Diane's wonderful wisdom, I wouldn't have known how to handle Nic to help him heal—with great kindness but a firm, trusting hand to build up his confidence. Just like a parent! Thank you so much, Diane! Here is a summary of my questions and her answers.

1. How intuitive/spiritual are horses vs. other animals?

Horses have a higher spiritual vibration than other animals (except the elephant, see Part II). Being spiritual simply means that human or horse has a closer connection and deeper conversation with the Universe or God. Horses have stronger personalities and greater intuitiveness than other animals, and they can relate more deeply to us. They are spiritual teachers, teaching where to place boundaries in our lives and also teaching us to have greater compassion for humans and horses alike. We need boundaries to stay focused on life's passionate pursuit and to keep unhealthy extraneous experiences or relationships from pulling us off track. And we definitely need greater compassion so that we can *feel* life—*feel* what others around us are really saying to us behind the words spoken. Then we can *feel* the energy around us in order to breathe in any angelic messages.

2. What is a horse's "big picture" purpose here on earth?

Horses are here to teach us wisdom and personal empowerment, especially to those humans who have been abused. They can help us reach way beyond the boundaries we have set for ourselves and dissolve the fear that keeps our feet set in concrete.

3. What does a horse want from his or her human?
Horses call us *their humans*, and they deeply desire that their humans understand their needs. They are searching for owners who are compassionate and loving so that they can be all they want to be, and all we want them to be.

    Author comment: There is a saying by the serious, compassionate horse person: "I just want to be all that my horse wants me to be." It's an everyday guideline for those of us who ride to keep in mind

The experts speak

while we are with a horse. What is he or she trying to say to me? What does he or she need? What do I need? How can we make this dance delicious?

4. What can we learn from a horse regarding living the fullest life possible?

Look into the eyes of a horse where his soul lives, and you will feel your answers to life in the beat of his heart. Ideas may come as words or an image in your head. The answers are all there. Equine listening comes naturally to horses—they are masters at it. You can divulge any problem to them, and they will give you answers. They are free spirits and want you to be the same. "Come play with me and we will have a ball, but be yourself, not someone else."

Horses can teach us to live the fullest life possible. We set too many limitations on ourselves. They strive to show us how not to give up. How to slow our pace down. They will mirror our emotions. If we are angry, they won't want to be with us. The same is true if we are on drugs or alcohol. They encourage us to overcome our challenges and limitations. They ask us to go the extra mile when we are on their backs or at their side.

5. What do you want the reader to know about animal communication?

Everyone can communicate with animals. It is easier for some because of their energetic make-up. Some people feel animals' and humans' vibrations more deeply than others and can translate those vibrations into words. They are inherently born with this gift just like a child who is a musical prodigy.

Animal communication is needed because it helps with the spiritual growth of humans. It teaches us compassion and the realization that life is so much larger than what we see before us. As humans' spirits expand, the animals' souls expand too, and the world's soul expands along with us. It's just like throwing a pebble in the lake and seeing the ripples. Such is spiritual expansion for humans. As humans become more soulfully in tune with the animal world, they become more compassionately alive and help the entire world expand as well.

6. What would you want the reader to know about your work?

"I do this work for the animals. I am helping humans with a better understanding of how to treat animals. They are in our trust, and it is our responsibility to help these animals grow, as we would our children. All of the animal kingdom is a great teacher. We must stop the suffering of all of the animals. Human egos are at fault. They use animals to elevate their egos. We, as keepers of the kingdom on earth, must have more compassion for all living things."

Diane Roadcap can be reached at this number or email address for a phone or in-person session: 703-719-5975, diane@animalstalktoo.com. Visit her website at www.animalstalktoo.com.

John in the infamous Equestrian Singles photo
(Courtesy of Scott Gearan)

CHAPTER 14

The angels continue to amaze

*Life is not measured by the number of breaths we take,
but by the moments that take our breath away.*
George Carlin

It was December 30, 2007, in Sarasota, Florida, and I heard a torturous yell from the bedroom, "Sue!" I dashed from the bathroom to find my husband, Bob Kipperman, lying back on the bed, eyes closed, and his lips losing color. There's a certain finality to the energy of one who has just died, and I could feel it. It was very still. Panic started to take over. I called 911, and they urgently guided me through heart compressions to try to bring him back to life. They told me to pull him off the bed in order to get him on the hard surface of the floor to perform CPR. I was doing compressions when the ambulance arrived downstairs in front of the condo building. It was Sunday, and the outside condo gate was locked. I threw on some clothes and flew downstairs to let them in. The EMTs took over to try and resuscitate Bob. I was numb and totally in shock.

I had been preparing for this day for more than ten years, but you are never ready for such a loss. Bob had cardiac sarcoidosis, which was a growth of scar tissue on the heart muscle and a very rare disease. He had excellent care, but I could tell from what he kept saying the last few years that he just wanted to give up. All the medications, the surgeries to place and replace the defibrillator/pacemaker, and just the general wear and tear of feeling awful took their toll. But you, as the spouse, are never prepared for the death of a loved one. I believe that we each choose our time to leave this earth, even if we are not consciously aware of our choice. Bob had been waiting from the first diagnosis of sarcoidosis to let go. He did not like being so dependent on others and feeling like a victim of life. Bob died on December 30 on his own terms, as it should be for each of us.

There was no funeral. Bob wanted a life celebration with cigars and champagne. Cigars and champagne it was! After celebrating Bob's life on January 7, 2008, with our family and dear friends at a wonderful Life Celebration party, I stumbled around each day not eating or sleeping. How could I go on? We had been married for twenty-eight years. I was all alone and did not know what to do next. I traveled often to visit my two children, Cathy and Chris, and their families outside of Washington, D.C., and Boston. After six months, in June 2008, I started to feel a little more like myself. I could even get on my horse, Skye, without the fear that I couldn't handle something unforeseen if it happened. I had lived in so much fear of Bob's potential death, and then after he passed, I was so scared that I couldn't handle life by myself. My friends were starting to encourage me to at least go out to dinner with them. They were wonderful. Slowly but surely, I started to gain back some weight (I had lost fifteen pounds), and started exercising again. There was life after tragedy.

After eleven months of sadness, loneliness started creeping in. I started thinking about finding someone to at least share a dinner with. It was so lonely being by myself every day. My friends started encouraging me to think about getting out. Dating? At sixty-five? Really! They suggested I look at online dating. What would it hurt, they said?

So, I got online to vet out the dating sites. I wanted to at least go to dinner with a man and feel like I was still a woman. The ten

The angels continue to amaze

years had really taken their toll—so much pain and fear. Now was a time to start fresh and look forward to a life of change and new challenges. So, to the dating sites I went. I chatted online with a few men, but we had little in common. I didn't want to play golf and then go out to dinner every night. I wanted to meet someone who loved horses as I did. I wanted so desperately to learn to ride better.

At sixty-five I felt a deep desire to get on with my dreams. So, wouldn't you know, a human angel, my friend Stephanie opened the door to the next phase of my life, www.equestriansingles.com. I logged in to check out Equestrian Singles. I was looking for someone who at least lived close to me in Sarasota, Florida. I found a very interesting guy in Ocala, Florida, but I never heard back from him. Maybe he had already found a new partner. Oh, well! Then, I decided to look at geography closer to my daughter, Cathy, in Ashburn, Virginia, near Washington, D.C. When I visited her, perhaps I could meet someone with horses, and we could ride together. Then, it happened!

I found a man living about two hours south of Cathy. I clicked on his profile, and when I saw his photo, my stomach lurched. I clicked off. I couldn't look at his photo. I waited about ten minutes and clicked on his profile again. I looked at him and felt my whole body vibrate. I knew he was someone special. My daughter googled his name and told me he was a retired military hero, a Vietnam veteran. (I am from a military background and knew what the Silver Star and the Distinguished Flying Cross meant.) He had horses and had been riding all his life. But that wasn't what was lighting me up—it was this man's persona, not his background. I stared at that photo over and over again. I was overwhelmed, and I hadn't even spoken to him yet. I had stumbled upon John Pighini and wanted to know everything I could about him.

It took me two days to contact him online via Equestrian Singles. I was *so* nervous. I finally sent him an email and introduced myself. He simply asked for my phone number. Now, I was really scared. What had I done? I was still in widow mode. I shouldn't even consider dating. But, there was something about John—I just couldn't let go.

It just so happened that John had seen my profile on Equestrian Singles, too, and was wondering who I was and what I was like. Was I really a horse person, or was I just pretending in the profile photo? (I had posted a photo of me on the back of my second horse, Bandit.) Little did he know, I talked a good game but had so much to learn about horses.

John called me three days later, and we talked for two hours. The first thing he asked me was, "Do you know what a PJ is?" I said, you mean pajamas? He said, "No, go look it up on the web." I did and was amazed. After all my years around the military, I had never heard of this Special Operations Air Force unit, Pararescue (PJs). PJs are trained to rescue troops behind enemy lines. They are highly proficient in both emergency medicine and combat tactics. Their job is to parachute/helicopter into "hot" zones of combat to rescue our troops who have been wounded. They also are trained in all types of weather and terrain rescue to help not only our combat troops but also civilians in life-threatening situations. (I spotlighted Pararescue in chapter 4.) Wow! Was I ever impressed!

We continued to talk for about a month before we decided to meet after Thanksgiving when I would be visiting my daughter in Virginia. I had been a widow for almost a year by that time. For some reason, I was not laden with guilt about meeting this man. I think Bob, watching from heaven, wanted me to get on with my life. It had been ten years of intense struggle with his illness. It was time for me to move on with the *change* and *challenges* that were coming my way.

We met on the Saturday after Thanksgiving in 2008, and I was never more in love at first sight than when I met John Pighini. Make no mistake, Bob Kipperman and I had a wonderful marriage, but it had become a caretaker and patient relationship, not a true partnership any longer. The minute I saw John's photo, I knew. That's why I was so scared and my stomach was doing flip-flops. It was as if the angels had taken me by the hand and led me to John Pighini. When I saw him in person, there was no doubt that this was the other half of my soul. I just knew, but I had to keep this secret to myself because he didn't know. We spent the weekend together, and from there it was long distance romance from Virginia to Florida for the next six months. We moved in together on Mother's Day, May 2009, into his home in Virginia where I could now have my horses in my own backyard. What a thrill! I could see them every day and love on them every day. I was in heaven.

Six months more of living together and renovating John's home to accommodate the two of us (both working at home) and five horses. We were married on October 4, 2009, with both of our families attending. What a blast! We had so much fun! And it has been an unbelievable blessing every day since then. To find deep love at age sixty-five is wonderfully enchanting and exciting. I am so appreciative of this extraordinary man, his kindness, and his love of life. John has taught me so much about living fearlessly. Don't say "no" just because you are scared. Feel the fear and do it anyway. Say "yes" to every opportunity that comes your way.

The angelic realm set this relationship up through my human angel friend, Stephanie, the Internet, and our horses. I do not believe in coincidences in life. I believe we each create our own reality with our thoughts and help from the Divine. Each day, in every way, the angels, human and ethereal, are there to help and guide us to live the life we so richly deserve. I am blessed in living that life!

For you the reader, the message I want most to convey is *never give up on your dreams.* They are your true reality. Keep them alive with your energy and thoughts. Focus on what lights you up and makes you feel fantastic. You are a magnetic being, and you will attract exactly what you are thinking. So, concentrate for those 17 seconds several times a day on what you deeply desire. It will come to you. And, always go through the door of the unknown that is offered to you from the Universe; the exhilarating experiences waiting for you will be electrifying!

Sue and John with our "kids"

The angels continue to amaze

John

Bob Wheeler
(Courtesy of Jamie Golden)

Epilogue

Life should not be a journey to the grave with the intention of arriving safely in an attractive and well preserved body, but rather to skid in sideways, champagne in one hand, strawberries in the other, body thoroughly used up, totally worn out and screaming WOO HOO— What a ride!
Hunter S. Thompson

Today, September 15, 2015, I am flying back home to Virginia from Reno, Nevada, having attended the "Life Celebration" of an extraordinary American hero, a retired US Air Force Pararescueman, Chief Master Sergeant Robert G. Wheeler. Bob received the Distinguished Flying Cross for heroism in Vietnam, the Airman's Medal, and several other Air Medals for life saving rescues. There were more than 500 people in the ballroom at the Incline Village/Lake Tahoe Hyatt Hotel to celebrate Bob's life. I had only just met Bob this past summer as he was a very close friend of my husband, John, during their twenty years in Pararescue. After their retirement from Pararescue, Bob and John stayed in very close contact for the next thirty years. The minute I met Bob, I knew he was an extraordinary human being who helped others believe in themselves just by the way he listened and the example he set.

Expect the Extraordinary

We were invited to Lake Tahoe for July 4th, which was a highlight event in Nevada with Lake Tahoe's "Red, White, and Tahoe Blue Celebration" that Bob orchestrated. He took care of every minute detail, from cocktail parties overlooking beautiful Lake Tahoe to Pararescuemen parachuting into the lake from a C130 airplane carrying the American flag, landing in the lake, and being picked up by an H-160 helicopter to demonstrate a water rescue. Wow, is all I can say! Every minute was filled with heart-warming events inviting 14,000 people on the beach to laugh, love, live, and be proud to be Americans.

From the moment you met Bob Wheeler, you just knew he was remarkable. He gathered people around him like bees to honey. Bob exuded leadership and confidence, even to those who did not have a military background. He wetted your appetite for a drink from his bottomless cup of passion for life. He brought together like-minded individuals who felt that life should be lived to the fullest, even if your time on earth might be limited.

Bob had idiopathic pulmonary fibrosis and was dying. From the moment he picked us up at the airport in July and I saw him struggling to breathe and glimpsed his many oxygen tanks in the backseat of the car, I knew he would only be with us a short time longer. He was still living life to the fullest and inviting his friends and family to do the same just by his example. Bob died September 4, 2015, in the University of Southern California Intensive Care Unit waiting for a lung transplant. He was #1 on the transplant list.

We all know people whom we admire. We want to be more like those people. Bob Wheeler was that type of admirable person. He lived his life from his heart. He lived his life full of love for his family and friends, but still was his own person exploring the nooks and crannies of what life had to offer. He wasn't concerned about what other people thought of him because it was more important that he challenged himself to accomplish all the things that gave

Epilogue

him joy. He loved his job in Pararescue, and later as a noted real estate broker.

As a decorated Pararescueman, Bob was awarded the Distinguished Flying Cross for his extremely hazardous rescue mission of a downed American pilot deep in enemy territory in Southeast Asia in 1970. Bob's mission aircraft received intense ground fire during the rescue, which he suppressed with his mini-gun from the tail ramp of the HH-53 helicopter.

Bob's career as a highly successful real estate broker in Incline Village, Nevada, (Lake Tahoe) brought him immense happiness. He was recognized as Citizen of the Year for Incline Village as well as Realtor® of the Year. His flourishing broker business garnered over $750,000,000 in lifetime sales.

The key phrase about Bob's careers is "loved his job." He wouldn't waste his time on something that didn't bring him great satisfaction. And he loved golf, playing it every chance he got. He loved the camaraderie that golf brought. People were Bob's currency in life. How many people could he help? How many could he mentor and encourage being all they could be? His path of leadership wasn't simply seen in the Air Force. He guided everyone he cared about. Even the questions he asked encouraged you to reach higher than what you thought you desired in your everyday living.

The stories that were told at his life celebration were extraordinary. Not only did he set up his daughters in real estate, he helped others begin new lives too, including his cleaning lady. When she did such a great job for him, he thought it best if he set her up in her own home and office cleaning business. And then there is the friend who asked for a loan from Bob to buy one boat to start a boating enterprise, and now he has twenty-five boats and an enormously lucrative venture. Bob always expected the extraordinary in life. *Expect the Extraordinary in your life!*

I am telling you this story because Bob Wheeler is the epitome of the heart of this book. I say this because when someone lives life in joy and deep appreciation of what is next, he or she is living a reflection of the Divine for each of us *to emulate*. *Expect the Extraordinary* isn't just about thrilling, life-saving stories; *it is about you*. What do you want your life to look like before you decide to leave this life?

The essence of this book is about welcoming change, change to grow and take chances, like Scott and Donnie. Scott, a Pararescueman, jumped out of airplanes to challenge greater personal freedom regardless of the possibility of danger. He now speaks to groups on how to overcome a fear of death and live a life of immense satisfaction. In Donnie's early years as a master herbalist, he was behind the counter at a local health food store dispensing advice on supplements. Today, he is a world-renowned holistic healer who receives invitations from the National Institute of Health, the Mayo Clinic, Johns Hopkins, and Moffitt Cancer Center, as well as other highly respected medical organizations, to speak and consult about his natural-healing practices. Each of these men sought out what gave them the greatest joy in life. Every time each of them was faced with a new challenge, they took it on. They welcomed new challenges.

Scott, Donnie, and Bob pursued paths to *celebrate* and *appreciate* all of life. You can too. Every time you feel an inner pull to investigate something new—read a book, talk to a friend, travel to a certain place, create a much thought-after change—act on it right then. That is *your* personal angelic connection tapping you on the shoulder to urge you to go forth and re-create your life.

Bob Wheeler has now become a guardian angel to his entourage of family and friends, as well as those who tap into his energy, as you may do as you read this book. He has been welcomed with open arms on the "other side." He lived his life to the fullest and left an indelible example for all of us to follow. Bob enjoyed the fruits of his earthly labors—money and material goods—but the true gift

Epilogue

he gave to me and others is an example of how to live life full out, never being affected by what others thought or said. Those of us who have glimpsed the other side want so desperately to pass along this exact message. You don't need to have had a near death experience, a life-threatening disease, or been robbed at gunpoint to know that there are heavenly and earthly angels to show you the way to living a grand life filled with gratitude and joy. When standing at the gates of the other side, we each will be asked, "Did you have joy and did you make a difference?"

In conclusion, I want to thank you, the reader, for being willing to *take a chance* to believe that you do not have to travel alone. You have all-loving angelic beings, animal guides, and human saints assigned just to you, to be with you on the ride of a lifetime. Just believe that these heavenly and earthly guides exist. I can sometimes feel the angelic messengers hovering over my right shoulder, giggling at my perceived struggles. You can feel them there, too. You can sometimes even get a glimpse of their fluttering wings out of the corner of your eye, waiting for you to come out and play with them in the great sandbox of life!

Wishing you a life of Extraordinary Expectations!

With love, light, and laughter,

Sue

Acknowledgments

I have so many wonderful people to thank. I will mention them here with an enormous thank you! They all know how very special they are in my life and in the yearlong creation of this book.

- Dr. Diane Chesson, my very trusted and brilliant editor who has encouraged me when I was lost and chastised me when I was lazy.
- Dunn+Associates: The highly creative force behind the cover and production of this book. Without their expertise and guidance, I would still be struggling with a concept. Thank you, Kathi and Hobie.
- Susan Niemi and John Kober, publishing consultants and editors for the amazing work they did on the final edit of this book.
- Dorie McClelland, interior designer, who turned this book into a creative masterpiece from simple written pages.
- My husband, John, who reminded me that it was time to write versus curling up in bed reading my thriller fiction. And, who ate nachos for dinner, a lot! Who was also an extraordinary editor. I love you so much, Sweetheart.
- To my adult children, who are my examples of living life on the edge and loving it. Love you, Chris and Cathy.

Expect the Extraordinary

- To my stepchildren, Lynne, Wendy, Todd: Love you all for being such shining examples of those who follow their dreams.
- John's daughter, Jonnie: Thank you and love you for never giving up. You are an inspiration to us all.
- R'Delle Anderson, a gifted intuitive, who has coached me all along the way with not only this book but all of my future dreams.

Resources

- Diane Chesson, PhD., literary editor extraordinaire: www.drdianechesson.com.
- Kathi Dunn, Hobie Hobart: Highly creative cover designers. www.dunn-design.com.
- Dorie McClelland: Interior design. www.springbookdesign.com
- Susan Niemi, John Kober: s.niemi@huffpublishing.com
- R'Delle Anderson: www.essentiallysoul.com. Gifted intuitive.
- Drs. McCormick: Institute of Conscious Awareness, www.horsesenseandthehumanheart.com. Nationally recognized psychologists in the field of equine assisted learning.
- Diane Roadcap: Exceptional animal communicator: www.animalstalktoo.com.
- Meredith Young Sowers, Dr. of Div.: The Stillpoint Foundation: World renown spiritual healer, teacher, and author: www.stillpoint.org.
- Donnie Yance: Internationally recognized natural healer, master herbalist and nutritionist: www.mederifoundation.org.

Sue and Bella

About the author

Sue found her passion for helping and guiding others when she left her sales and marketing career in New York City and joined Avon, Inc., to help launch their new division, Lifedesigns. Lifedesigns was founded on the premise that women could be all they desired to be with a little help from other women who were already on their own paths of passion. Lifedesigns conducted workshops all over the country, helping women find their *light*, their passion. From there, Sue went on to study transformational coaching at David Gershon and Gail Straub's Empowerment Institute. She then became certified as an Intuitive Healer and studied with Dr. Meredith Young-Sowers at The Stillpoint Institute where she later taught the intuitive healing curriculum.

After twenty-five years in corporate America, Sue realized that there had to be more to her life than just earning money. She was constantly exploring new paths. She became a Life Transitional Coach and Change Agent after graduating from The Stillpoint Institute. Sue now offers "Creativity Life Coaching: Helping Create Lives of Positive Change" that guides others onto a new life path of:
- Intuitive awareness
- Living their uniqueness
- Learning the courage of change
- Learning to leave behind the safety of sameness, the protection of the past, or being stuck in loss

In order to expand her personal bond with the angelic world, Sue searched for fifteen years to find other avenues of spiritual expansion. She found an extension of her life as a spiritual seeker and teacher through the soul of a horse—Skye, a self-determined mare. Knowing that this horse was leading Sue on an entirely new path of self-exploration, she went on to study with Dr. Deborah McCormick, one of three Drs. McCormick who founded The Institute of Conscious Awareness in San Antonio, Texas. Discovering the healing personalities of horses through Dr. McCormick has given Sue another avenue of personal expansion to offer her clients at her and John's ranch, Livin' the Dream Ranch, in Virginia and Florida. She is also certified as an Eagala Equine Specialist, one who asks the horse to partner with a human for healing of emotional and physical challenges.

Today, Sue is a much sought-after speaker, talking to audiences about expanding their fearlessness in living the life they most desire. She counsels her clients by phone or in person at the ranch. She can be reached at sue@suepighini.com.